HARCOURT

Math

Practice
Workbook

Grade 5

Harcourt

Orlando • Boston • Dallas • Chicago • San Diego
www.harcourtschool.com

CONTENTS

Understand Place Value

Write the value of the **boldfaced** digit.

1. **3**,645

2. 3**4**

3. **7**98,000

_____   _____   _____

4. 6**4**,530

5. **8**92

6. **6**02,456

_____   _____   _____

Write each number in expanded form and word form.

7. 23,645 _____

_____

8. 990,104 _____

_____

9. 7,828 _____

_____

Write each number in standard form.

10. $40,000 + 2,000 + 600 + 80 + 2$

11. thirty-five thousand, forty-two

_____   _____

Mixed Review

12. $17 + 98$ _____

13. $85 - 58$ _____

14. 56×7 _____

15. 25×5 _____

16. 95×2 _____

17. 11×2 _____

18. 237
    $+ \ 63$

19. 468
    $- \ \ 9$

20. 314
    $+ \ \ 9$

21. 324
    $- \ 32$

22. 418
    $- \ 21$

23. 603
    $- \ 27$

24. 257
    $+ \ \ 5$

25. 354
    $+236$

26. 716
    $+931$

27. 480
    -139

Millions and Billions

Write each number in standard form.

1. thirty-two million, ten thousand one

    _____

2. three hundred two billion, sixty million, sixty-six thousand, nine hundred

    _____

Write the value of the **boldfaced** digit.

3. **1**89,612,357

    _____

4. 521,**8**74,394

    _____

5. **3**,794,216,055

    _____

Write each number in two different ways.

6. 125,740,689 _____

    _____

    _____

7. 200,403,926 _____

    _____

    _____

8. 5,248,663,711 _____

    _____

    _____

9. A bowl holds 100 peanuts. How many bowls would hold a million peanuts?

    _____

10. If you save 10¢ a day, how many days would it take to save a million cents?

    _____

Mixed Review

Write the factors.

11. 15 _____

12. 36 _____

13. 27 _____

Compare Numbers

Start at the left. Name the first place-value position where the
digits differ. Name the greater number.

1. 1,799,347;

1,797,221

_____

_____

2. 3,555,782;

2,639,221

_____

_____

3. 97,145,346;

97,245,375

_____

_____

4. 670,256,112;

569,247,221

_____

_____

5. 34,910,023;

34,910,295

_____

_____

6. 83,945,203;

82,943,290

_____

_____

7. 823,579,044;

823,579,043

_____

_____

8. 749,566,001;

759,566,000

_____

_____

9. 56,239,448;

56,217,456

_____

_____

10. 967,442,011;

967,442,021

_____

_____

11. 326,599,675;

326,738,902

_____

_____

12. 5,266,903;

5,266,993

_____

_____

Compare. Write $<$, $>$, or $=$ in each ◯.

13. 345,922 ◯ 34,592

14. 275,669,128 ◯ 275,669,129

15. 44,576,493 ◯ 44,577,497

16. 67,387 ◯ 67,256

17. 55,377,294 ◯ 55,377,294

18. 935,771,220 ◯ 935,771,212

19. 456,197,203 ◯ 456,197,203

20. 1,366,792 ◯ 1,266,457

21. 77,032,665 ◯ 77,932,440

22. 2,767,394,201 ◯ 2,769,341,222

23. 811,564,007 ◯ 811,566,290

24. 67,294,007 ◯ 67,294,007

Mixed Review

25. $48 \div 4$ _____

26. $75 + 19$ _____

27. $55 - 29$ _____

28. 7×8 _____

Name _____

Order Numbers

Order from greatest to least.

1. 2,647; 217,553; 23,667

_____

2. 295,254; 386,407; 385,245

_____

3. 16,450; 16,399; 16,576;

_____

4. 2,735; 28,362; 532

_____

5. 1,750,439; 1,750,419; 1,750,506

_____

6. 5,064; 5,245; 6,001

_____

7. 676,259; 733,157; 7,892

_____

8. 669,345,201; 669,345,903; 668,544,201

_____

Order from least to greatest.

9. 7,674; 7,773; 7,978

_____

10. 690,699; 275,789; 544,266

_____

11. 1,300,546; 1,259,708; 1,259,456

_____

12. 43,857; 45,019; 44,777

_____

13. 5,060,560; 5,052,300; 5,053,980

_____

14. 87,315; 97,229; 78,999

_____

15. 56,275,988; 56,275,703; 56,295,148

_____

16. 453,097,111; 473,095,477; 452,555,439

_____

Mixed Review

17. 8×8 _____
18. $48 \div 8$ _____
19. $49 - 16$ _____
20. $57 + 19$ _____

21. $62 - 44$ _____
22. 5×12 _____
23. $84 + 12$ _____
24. 45×2 _____

25. Write nine billion, seven hundred million, forty-five thousand, three hundred six in standard form. _____

Problem Solving Skill

Use a Table

For 1–3, use the States table.

1. Which state has the greatest population?

   _____

2. Which state has a population of eight million when rounded to the nearest million?

   _____

3. Which states have populations greater than 10,000,000?

   _____

STATES	
Name	**Population**
Arkansas	2,538,303
California	32,666,550
Georgia	7,642,207
Illinois	12,045,326

For 4–6, use the California Cities table.

4. Order the cities from greatest to least population.

   _____

   _____

CALIFORNIA CITIES	
City	**Population**
San Diego	1,110,549
Los Angeles	3,485,398
Long Beach	429,433
San Francisco	723,959

5. Which city has a population of about one million?

   _____

6. Which city's population is about 300,000 more than Long Beach's population?

   _____

Mixed Review

Compare. Write $<$, $>$, or $=$ in each $\bigcirc$.

7. 563 $\bigcirc$ 653   8. 975 $\bigcirc$ 946   9. 432 $\bigcirc$ 412

10. 294 $\bigcirc$ 314   11. 506 $\bigcirc$ 560   12. 813 $\bigcirc$ 381

Tenths and Hundredths

Write as a decimal and a fraction or mixed number.

1.

2.

3.

_____   _____   _____

4. 5 + 0.4

5. 0.8 + 0.01

6. 7 + 0.9 + 0.03

_____   _____   _____

7. sixty-five hundredths

8. four and three tenths

9. seven and twenty-two hundredths

_____   _____   _____

Write the missing decimal in each pattern. Describe the pattern.

10. 0.15, 0.30, 0.45, ☐, 0.75

11. 1.12, 1.04, 0.96, ☐, 0.80, 0.72

_____   _____

12. 2.07, 2.14, ☐, 2.28

13. 0.1, 0.5, ☐, 1.3, 1.7

_____   _____

Mixed Review

14. 99 ÷ 3

15. 11 × 7

16. 292 + 308

17. 934 − 349

_____   _____   _____   _____

18. Write five billion, three hundred fifty-seven million in standard form.

19. Write the value of the boldfaced digit in 4,5**9**3,678,002.

_____   _____

Order from least to greatest.

20. 518,808; 518,388; 518,838

21. 64,460,144; 64,660,114; 64,604,111

_____   _____

Thousandths and Ten-Thousandths

Write each decimal in expanded form, in word form, and as a fraction.

1. 2.089

_____

_____

_____

2. 4.1967

_____

_____

_____

3. 3.504

_____

_____

_____

4. 0.6045

_____

_____

_____

Write in standard or expanded form.

5. fifteen thousandths

_____

6. one and forty-seven ten-
thousandths

_____

7. 1.808

_____

8. 7.0541

_____

9. 2.638

_____

10. 3.8279

_____

Write in word form.

11. 4.0017 _____

12. 12.683 _____

13. 0.5983 _____

14. 31.234 _____

Mixed Review

15. 789 + 426

16. 710 − 268

17. 56 ÷ 7

18. 39 × 4

_____

Name _____

Equivalent Decimals

Write *equivalent* or *not equivalent* to describe each pair of decimals.

1. 6.4 and 6.40

2. 2.08 and 2.008

3. 5.090 and 5.09

4. 1.0050 and 1.005

5. 3.006 and 3.060

6. 0.07 and 0.70

Write an equivalent decimal for each number.

7. 1.2

8. 3.71

9. 0.060

10. 6.200

11. 3.450

12. 4.15

13. 2.4

14. 7.30

Write the two decimals that are equivalent.

15. 3.01050
   3.01005
   3.0105

16. 0.005
   0.050
   0.0050

17. 0.101
   0.1010
   0.1001

18. 2.808
   2.8008
   2.80080

Mixed Review

19. 1,235 − 465

20. 5,605 + 2,487

21. 12 × 8

22. 42 ÷ 6

23. Write 42,765,249 in word form.

24. Write six and seven thousand, four hundred thirty-three ten-thousandths in standard form.

Compare and Order Decimals

Write <, >, or = in each ◯. Use the number line.

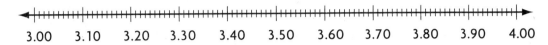

3.00 3.10 3.20 3.30 3.40 3.50 3.60 3.70 3.80 3.90 4.00

1. 3.622 ◯ 3.262   **2.** 3.201 ◯ 3.021   **3.** 3.597 ◯ 3.63

4. 3.309 ◯ 3.42   **5.** 3.545 ◯ 3.455   **6.** 3.152 ◯ 3.251

Write <, >, or = in each ◯.

7. 0.25 ◯ 0.23   **8.** 46.564 ◯ 46.652   **9.** 7.21 ◯ 7.210

10. 627.35 ◯ 627.53   **11.** 368.58 ◯ 368.85   **12.** 237.524 ◯ 237.254

13. 736.54 ◯ 736.540   **14.** 16.2 ◯ 16.200   **15.** 878.787 ◯ 878.878

Order from least to greatest.

16. 7.11, 7.09, 7.07   **17.** 12.54, 12.45, 12.65   **18.** 3.020, 3.002, 3.200

_____   _____   _____

19. 17.560, 17.065, 17.056   **20.** 2.654, 2.546, 2.456, 2.465

_____   _____

Mixed Review

21. 72 ÷ 8   **22.** 1,630   **23.**   9   **24.**   1,498
                          − 472   × 6   + 2,645

_____   _____   _____   _____

25. Write six and twenty-seven   **26.** Write 8.1406 in word form.
hundredths as a decimal and a
fraction.   _____

_____   _____

27. Write ninety-five million, two   **28.** Write 31,125,624.6 in expanded
hundred six thousand, eleven in   form.
standard form.

_____   _____

_____   _____

Problem Solving Skill

Draw Conclusions

Can the conclusion be drawn from the information given?
Write *yes, no,* or *maybe.* Explain your choice.

At the class party, Mr. Conner asked his math students to guess how many pennies were in a jar. The five students whose guesses were the closest to the actual number were: Charles 375, Juan 350, Carmen 360, Ann 373, and Bill 395. There was only one winner and that student missed by 5 pennies.

1. There were more than 344 pennies in the jar.

_____

_____

_____

2. The actual number of pennies was between 350 and 395.

_____

_____

_____

3. If Bill is the winner, the actual number of pennies was 400.

_____

_____

_____

4. The actual number of pennies was not 355.

_____

_____

_____

Mixed Review

Solve.

5. Sal and Alice planted trees for the Forestry Service. Last weekend Sal planted 113 trees, and Alice planted 96 trees. How many more trees did Sal plant than Alice?

_____

6. Cheryl wants to put a border around her window. The window is 3 feet wide and 5 feet high. How much border does she need to go around the window?

_____

Round Whole Numbers

Round each number to the place of the **bold-faced** digit.

1. 105,509   2. **7**,485,762   3. 34,9**8**8   4. 47,**5**67   5. 61,**2**44

_____ _____ _____ _____ _____

6. 72,**8**32   7. **9**,355,722   8. 5**6**3,044   9. **4**28,995   10. 27,549,1**0**5

_____ _____ _____ _____ _____

Round 73,127,849 to the place named.

11. millions   12. tens   13. ten thousands

_____   _____   _____

14. thousands   15. hundred thousands   16. ten millions

_____   _____   _____

Name the place to which each number was rounded.

17. 76,145 to 76,000   18. 495,346 to 500,000   19. 5,927 to 5,930

_____   _____   _____

20. 4,901,216 to 4,901,200 21. 9,347,002 to 9,350,000 22. 1,555,299 to 2,000,000

_____   _____   _____

Mixed Review

23. $482 + 785$ 24. $761 - 282$ 25. 9×7 26. $36 \div 6$

_____   _____   _____   _____

27. Order the decimals 0.435, 0.043, and 0.450 from greatest to least.

28. Write the value of the bold-faced digit: 2.05**4**1.

29. Write 16.8072 in expanded form.

_____   _____   _____

_____   _____   _____

Estimate Sums and Differences

Estimate by rounding.

1. 267,335 + 492,177	**2.** 539,369 + 91,136	**3.** 555,411 − 202,302	**4.** 6,110,785 − 3,385,142
_____	_____	_____	_____
5. 1,665,499 + 433,801	**6.** 838,624 − 157,240	**7.** 476,428 + 224,800	**8.** 7,587,057 − 3,569,882
_____	_____	_____	_____

9. 324,966 + 474,022   **10.** 828,477 − 498,549   **11.** 546,239 − 196,874

_____   _____   _____

12. 495,106 − 271,392   **13.** 3,428,687 + 5,680,952   **14.** 281,978 + 44,477

_____   _____   _____

Estimate to compare. Write > or < for each ◯.

15. 65,322 + 24,801 ◯ 69,595 + 32,783   _____

16. 402,602 − 159,600 ◯ 398,011 − 274,261   _____

17. 751,493 − 112,302 ◯ 775,029 − 272,886   _____

18. 622,367 + 92,945 ◯ 840,926 − 114,609   _____

19. 85,493 − 32,302 ◯ 75,029 − 42,886   _____

20. 473,163 + 50,498 ◯ 502,931 + 83,641   _____

Mixed Review

21. Order the numbers 3.01; 3.011; 3.0012; 3.120; and 3.110 from greatest to least.

_____

22. Write 53.2818 in word form.

_____

_____

Add and Subtract Whole Numbers

Find the sum or difference. Estimate to check.

1.　3,964
　+ 2,489
　_____

2.　12,033
　− 7,566
　_____

3.　9,209
　− 7,644
　_____

4.　5,439
　+ 4,053
　_____

5.　17,848
　+ 24,189
　_____

6.　45,178
　+ 18,433
　_____

7.　7,428
　− 4,119
　_____

8.　39,702
　+ 3,589
　_____

9.　96,260
　− 45,779
　_____

10.　21,816
　+ 42,112
　_____

11.　61,422
　+ 28,919
　_____

12.　42,631
　+ 9,687
　_____

13. 226 + 339 + 498

14. 7,018 − 965

15. 26,253 + 13,348

16. 59,607 − 23,423

17. 15,046 − 4,699

18. 41,212 + 19,309

19. 1,406 + 871 + 521

20. 91,233 − 38,877

21. 612 + 964 + 1,107

Mixed Review

22. 72 ÷ 8

23. 12 × 6

24. 8 × 8

25. 48 ÷ 12

26. Name the greater number: 5,675,893 or 5,675,983.

27. Write thirty-nine and three thousand, nine hundred forty-seven ten-thousandths in standard form.

28. Round 5,347,299 to the nearest ten thousand.

29. Write <, >, or = in ◯.

418.8342 ◯ 418.8432

Choose a Method

Find the sum or difference. Estimate to check.

1. 1,216,783 + 3,876,121	**2.** 5,698,522 − 4,301,056	**3.** 5,460,900 − 652,294	**4.** 9,056,357 − 410,652

5. 5,677,398 + 2,211,545	**6.** 9,045,063 − 904,506	**7.** 2,260,577 + 7,739,533	**8.** 8,324,756 + 593,664

9. 8,366,645 − 2,633,193	**10.** 6,761,250 + 8,488,329	**11.** 31,234,329 + 48,283,517	**12.** 19,880,441 − 7,582,299

13. 6,088,197 − 2,870,034   **14.** 2,673,452 + 6,333,247   **15.** 8,986,899 − 3,545,999

16. 7,005,088 + 681,374   **17.** 4,141,114 − 371,173   **18.** 5,027,405 + 3,765,323

Mixed Review

19. Order the decimals 1.0450, 1.0045, 1.1045, 1.0050, 1.0004 from least to greatest.

20. Write the decimal 498.036 in word form.

21. Round 4,743,996 to the place of the bold-faced digit.

22. Write 2,000,000 + 600,000 + 8,000 + 300 + 30 + 0.08 in standard form.

23. Name the place to which the following number was rounded: 843,907 to 844,000.

24. Write > or < for $\bigcirc$.

98,311 − 40,298 $\bigcirc$ 15,518 + 44,982

Problem Solving Strategy

Use Logical Reasoning

Use logical reasoning to solve.

1. Mark, Christina, Nick, and Julio each bought a different color pencil at the bookstore. The colors were blue, red, yellow, and green. Nick's and Julio's pencils are colors on the United States' flag. Christina's pencil is bright like the sun, and Julio's is the color of the sky. Which pencil did each person buy?

_____

_____

_____

2. Five students, Maria, Ivan, Leah, Julie, and Scott measured each other's heights for health class. The heights are 42, 39, 41, 37, and 39 inches. Julie is 2 inches shorter than Leah. Maria is 1 inch shorter than Scott and 2 inches taller than Leah. How tall is each student?

_____

_____

_____

Mixed Review

3. Mari scored twice as many points in the second half of the basketball game as she did in the first half. She scored 24 points in the second half. How many points did Mari score in the whole game?

_____

4. The Hobbs family had to travel 856 miles to return home after their vacation. In the past two days they have traveled 413 miles and 269 miles. How many more miles does the Hobbs family have to travel?

_____

5. Marsha bought a mountain bike on sale for $112.56 plus $6.75 tax. The regular price was $149.99 including tax. How much did Marsha save?

_____

6. Last winter it snowed 12.9 cm in December, 17.4 cm in January, 16.9 cm in February, and 8.6 cm in March. In which month did the most snow fall?

_____

Name _____

Round Decimals

Round each number to the place of the **boldfaced** digit.

1. 3.2**7**6
2. 12.**6**3
3. 0.4**8**70
4. 15.3**8**47
5. 8.**6**9

_____ _____ _____ _____ _____

6. 20.5**9**56
7. 11.**3**23
8. 7.9**0**93
9. **4**.2899
10. 7.5**4**75

_____ _____ _____ _____ _____

Round 4.5227 to the place named.

11. tenths
12. thousandths
13. hundredths
14. ones

_____ _____ _____ _____

Name the place to which each number was rounded.

15. 12.35 to 12.4
16. 0.4288 to 0.429
17. 9.462 to 9.46

_____ _____ _____

18. 5.0999 to 5
19. 4.6837 to 4.68
20. 6.29385 to 6.294

_____ _____ _____

Mixed Review

21. 8
×6

22. 9
×4

23. 7
×3

24. 6
×6

25. 9
×7

26. Write 7.0051 in word form.

27. Write an equivalent decimal for 6.0250.

_____

28. Order 2.37, 2.73, 2.46, and 2.64 from least to greatest.

29. 1,245 − 224

30. 2
×5

31. 8
×8

32. 3
×6

33. 9
×5

34. 6
×7

Estimate Decimal Sums and Differences

Estimate the sum or difference. Tell which method
you used.

1. $\begin{array}{r} 6.45 \\ -\ 2.81 \end{array}$	2. $\begin{array}{r} 7.32 \\ -\ 5.14 \end{array}$	3. $\begin{array}{r} \$7.68 \\ +\ 3.52 \end{array}$	4. $\begin{array}{r} 18.07 \\ +\ 11.66 \end{array}$	5. $\begin{array}{r} 27.36 \\ -\ 15.04 \end{array}$

Estimate the sum or difference to the nearest tenth.

6. $\begin{array}{r} 1.285 \\ +\ 0.822 \end{array}$	7. $\begin{array}{r} 2.843 \\ +\ 7.158 \end{array}$	8. $\begin{array}{r} 4.060 \\ -\ 3.724 \end{array}$	9. $\begin{array}{r} 6.341 \\ -\ 1.636 \end{array}$	10. $\begin{array}{r} 2.578 \\ -\ 0.372 \end{array}$

Estimate to compare. Write $<$ or $>$ in each $\bigcirc$.

11. $7.21 - 5.56 \bigcirc 6.89 - 2.34$ 12. $4.73 + 3.29 \bigcirc 5.32 + 2.39$

13. $9.213 + 4.764 \bigcirc 8.345 + 6.754$ 14. $36.84 - 15.49 \bigcirc 58.94 - 37.99$

15. $45.76 + 21.84 \bigcirc 32.98 + 34.05$ 16. $52.85 + 34.76 \bigcirc 46.34 + 39.82$

17. $9.034 - 4.571 \bigcirc 7.562 - 2.199$ 18. $6.045 - 2.374 \bigcirc 8.461 - 5.921$

Mixed Review

19. Write an equivalent decimal for
13.48.

_____

20. Round 34.6487 to the nearest
hundredth.

_____

21. Find the value of n in
$47 + n = 185$.

_____

22. Evaluate $125 + n$ if $n = 67$.

_____

23. Which 5 has the least value?

    A 2.519   **C** 10.259

    B 5.189   **D** 13.075

24. Which number is twelve million,
two thousand written in standard
form?

    F 12,200,000   **H** 1,202,200

    G 12,002,000   **J** 1,200,200

Add and Subtract Decimals

Find the sum or difference. Estimate to check.

1. 2.7
    + 1.1

2. 7.568
    + 3.405

3. 42.35
    6.81
    + 9.47

4. 11.79
    + 15.02

5. 13.75
    4.31
    + 2.10

6. 7.5
    + 2.3

7. 6.38
    8.12
    + 13.52

8. 4.054
    + 7.285

9. 22.35
    + 11.86

10. 3.817
    6.194
    + 5.417

11. 8.59
    − 2.34

12. 9.8
    − 2.3

13. 6.27
    − 0.83

14. 12.362
    − 8.18

15. 10.98
    − 1.29

16. 3.1
    − 1.7

17. 6.14
    − 4.81

18. 15.09
    − 8.73

19. 39.47
    − 22.29

20. 68.17
    − 32.51

21. 22.12 − 6.78

22. 21.599 − 17.369

23. 8.376 − 2.109

_____

_____

_____

24. 10.05 + 2.78

25. 678 + 3.410

26. 8.9 + 7.25 + 5.42

_____

_____

_____

Mixed Review

27. Round 24.579 to the nearest hundredth.

28. 45,681 + 98,810

_____

_____

29. Order 12.1, 12.34, 12.43, and 12.5 from greatest to least.

30. Which is greater, twenty-seven thousandths or fourteen hundredths?

_____

_____

31. 739
    621
    + 667

32. 7,232
    946
    + 31

33. 2,780
    9,621
    +3,221

34. 8,869
    4,500
    + 399

Zeros in Subtraction

Find the difference.

1. 2.5 − 0.8	2. 3.4 − 3.1	3. 2.04 − 1.7	4. 3.6 − 2.7	5. 3.5 − 1.04

6. 1.6 − 0.8	7. 4.8 − 4.2	8. 3.07 − 2.8	9. 4.2 − 3.8	10. 6.7 − 2.02

11. 3.87 − 1.362	12. 2.7 − 1.824	13. 5.426 − 2.56	14. 12.507 − 4.315	15. 10.069 − 2.253

16. 4.68 − 2.157	17. 3.2 − 2.451	18. 7.264 − 3.49	19. 16.852 − 8.23	20. 17.57 − 13.154

21. $2.06 − 1.17 =$ _____   **22.** $1.7 − 0.763 =$ _____   **23.** $2.85 − 1.9 =$ _____

24. $3.7 − 2.68 =$ _____   **25.** $2.4 − 1.468 =$ _____   **26.** $3.1 − 2.51 =$ _____

27. $3.68 − 1.892 =$ _____   **28.** $5.2 − 3.181 =$ _____   **29.** $6.42 − 3.374 =$ _____

30. $4.21 − 2.362 =$ _____   **31.** $7.3 − 4.226 =$ _____   **32.** $5.69 − 2.473 =$ _____

Mixed Review

For 33–35, use the table.

33. The maximum speeds of animals over one-quarter mile varies greatly. What is the difference between the fastest and the slowest animal?

_____

34. How much faster is a greyhound than a human?

_____

SPEEDS OF ANIMALS	
Animal	**Speed**
Quarter horse	47.5 mph
Greyhound	39.35 mph
Human	27.89 mph
Snail	0.03 mph

35. In the snail's speed, what is the place value of the 3?

_____

Name _____

Problem Solving Skill

Estimate or Find Exact Answer

Decide whether you need an exact answer or an estimate. Then solve.

1. Ben received $10.00 for doing chores. He wants to buy some cards for $2.89, an action figure for $4.99, and a comic book for $1.79. Does he have enough to pay for all three items?

2. Yasmin received $50.00 for her birthday. She wants to buy a sweater for $13.99, a necklace for $14.95, and shoes for $19.98. How much change will she receive?

Kathy wants to buy some roses for $6.99, some potting soil for $3.98, and a ceramic pot for $7.95. She has $20.00.

3. Which question about Kathy's shopping can be answered with an estimate?
   A Does she have enough money for all 3 things?
   B How much will she pay in all?
   C How much change will she get?
   D Which item costs the least?

4. Which question represents Kathy's change?

   F $18.92 − $14.94 = $3.98
   G $6.99 + $3.98 + $7.95 = $18.92
   H $20 − $18.92 = $1.08
   J $20 − $1.08 = $18.92

Mixed Review

Solve.

5. Walt bought a CD player on sale for $99.95 plus $4.99 tax. The regular price was $149.99 including tax. How much did Walt save?

6. Emma spent $4 on cards and $18 on a sweater. Emma has $9 left. How much did Emma begin with?

7. In an even 2-digit number, the second digit is 3 times the first. What is the number?

8. Don is a cashier. When he calculates the amount of change, does he want an estimate or the exact answer?

Expressions and Variables

Write an expression. Find the value.

1. Mark had 6 books. He bought 5 more.

   _____

2. Sara baked 9 cupcakes. Her sister ate 3 of them.

   _____

3. Lillian got 3 letters in the mail. The next day she got 7 more.

   _____

4. Luke had 15 grapes in his lunch. He gave away 4 of them.

   _____

Write an expression with a variable. Explain what the variable represents.

5. TJ had 14 pet fish. He bought some more.

   _____

   _____

6. Alex picked 25 apples. He ate some.

   _____

   _____

Find the value of the expression.

7. $n + 37$ if n is 16

   _____

8. $234 + n$ if n is 66

   _____

For 9–10, choose the expression for each situation.

9. Joy rode down 5 floors on the elevator, and then rode up 3 floors.

   A $f - 5 + 3$ **C** $5 + 3 = f$

   B $f + 5 - 3$ **D** $f - 5 = 3$

10. Kim ate 3 of the 12 cookies, and then baked some more.

    F $3 + 12 + n$ **H** $12 - n - 3$

    G $12 - 3 + n$ **J** $9 + 3 + n$

Mixed Review

11. Use mental math to find the sum.
    $10 + 60 + 200 + 1{,}000$

    _____

12. Write a number between 1.0 and 1.4

    _____

Name _____

Write Equations

Write an equation. Explain what the variable represents.

1. Rick wants to read 52 books this year. He has already read 24 books. How many more should he read?

_____

_____

2. Jon saw 24 animals at the pet store. Fourteen were dogs and 3 were hamsters. How many other kinds of animals did he see?

_____

_____

3. There were 38 students in the choir. After 3 of the students moved away and 10 new students joined, how many students were in choir?

_____

_____

4. The buses departed with 39 students aboard. There were 32 students who waited for another bus. How many students are riding the buses?

_____

_____

5. Seven people joined the soccer team. The rest joined the softball team. There were 20 people that joined either the soccer or soft-ball team. How many people joined the softball team?

_____

_____

6. The theater group performed on Friday and Saturday nights. Three hundred and twenty four attended on Friday, and 33 more attended on Saturday. How many people saw the show?

_____

_____

On a separate sheet of paper, write a problem for the equation. State what the variable n represents.

7. $54 - n = 24$ 8. $n + 20 = 70$ 9. $5 + n - 3 = 10$

10. $4 + n = 12$ 11. $80 + n = 100$ 12. $n + 36 = 80$

Mixed Review

13. $23 + 12$ _____ 14. $56 + 12$ _____ 15. $73 + 12$ _____ 16. $90 - 80$ _____

17. $34 - 23$ _____ 18. $15 + 73$ _____ 19. $45 - 34$ _____ 20. $23 + 32$ _____

Solve Equations

Write which of the numbers 4, 8, or 12 is the solution of the equation.

1. $6 + n = 14$ 2. $40 - n = 28$ 3. $n + 58 = 62$ 4. $n - 6 = 6$

_____   _____   _____   _____

Use mental math to solve each equation. Check your solution.

5. $23 + n = 30$ 6. $100 - n = 60$ 7. $30 + n = 50$ 8. $n - 10 = 5$

_____   _____   _____   _____

Solve the equation. Check your solution.

9. $29 - n = 22$ 10. $n + 15 = 55$ 11. $60 - n = 2$ 12. $14 + n = 20$

_____   _____   _____   _____

13. $7 + n = 16$ 14. $42 - n = 26$ 15. $80 - n = 69$ 16. $6 + n = 32$

_____   _____   _____   _____

17. $46 + n = 59$ 18. $n - 16 = 9$ 19. $33 - n = 14$ 20. $(n - 5) + 8 = 23$

_____   _____   _____   _____

21. $25 + n = 40$ 22. $16 + n = 26$ 23. $26 - n = 9$ 24. $11 + (7 + n) = 24$

_____   _____   _____   _____

Mixed Review

25. What place value is the digit 7 in the number 43.567? _____

26. Order the numbers 4.578; 3.67, and 3.792 from
    least to greatest.

_____

27. $\begin{array}{r} 37{,}549 \\ + 26{,}385 \\ \hline \end{array}$ 28. $\begin{array}{r} 364{,}339 \\ - 235{,}188 \\ \hline \end{array}$ 29. $\begin{array}{r} \$31.04 \\ - 16.85 \\ \hline \end{array}$ 30. $\begin{array}{r} 34{,}600 \\ + 18{,}396 \\ \hline \end{array}$

31. $\begin{array}{r} 17.201 \\ - 12.009 \\ \hline \end{array}$ 32. $\begin{array}{r} 130.7907 \\ - 59.6010 \\ \hline \end{array}$ 33. $\begin{array}{r} 819.27 \\ + 222.35 \\ \hline \end{array}$ 34. $\begin{array}{r} 167.31 \\ + 49.99 \\ \hline \end{array}$

Name _____

Use Addition Properties

Name the addition property used in each equation.

1. $(3 + 1) + 6 = 3 + (1 + 6)$

2. $20 + 5 = 5 + 20$

3. $427 + 0 = 427$

4. $50 + (2 + 3) = (50 + 2) + 3$

5. $8 + 0 = 8$

6. $12 + 4 = 4 + 12$

7. $1.5 + (8.5 + 6) = (1.5 + 8.5) + 6$

8. $3{,}486 + 0 = 3{,}486$

Find the value of *n*. Identify the addition property used.

9. $3 + 12 = n + 3$

10. $0 + n = 49$

11. $(23 + 4) + 2 = 23 + (4 + n)$

12. $15.5 + (3.5 + 10) = (15.5 + n) + 10$

13. $58{,}454 + n = 58{,}454$

14. $14 + 16 = 16 + n$

Name the addition property used in each equation.

15. $c + 0 = c$

16. $a + b = b + a$

17. $x + (y + z) = (x + y) + z$

18. $n + r = r$

Mixed Review

19. 34×3 _____

20. 45×2 _____

21. $12 \times 2 \times 4$ _____

22. 45×4 _____

23. 67×2 _____

24. 78×12 _____

Name _____

Problem Solving Skill

Use a Formula

Use a formula to solve.

1. Maria's classroom is 22 feet long and 25 feet wide. How much paper is needed to make a border around the entire classroom?

_____

2. The perimeter of a pentagon is 94 yards. The sides measure 10 yards, 15 yards, 22 yards, 30 yards, and n yards. What is the measurement of the fifth side?

_____

3. Find the perimeter of a triangle. The sides measure 8 feet, 6 feet, and 6 feet.

_____

4. The school's rectangular garden is 12 feet long and 14 feet wide. How much fence is needed to enclose the garden?

_____

Margie walks a total of 15 miles per week. She walks a total of 6 days per week.

5. Which shows how to find the number of miles she walks per day?

   A $15 \times 6 = n$ **C** $15 + n = 6$

   B $15 \div 6 = n$ **D** $15 - 6 = n$

6. What does n equal in problem 5?

   F 9 miles **H** 2.3 miles

   G 2.5 miles **J** 90 miles

Mixed Review

7. Write an expression for this sentence: Mike had 15 potato chips and gave some away. _____

8. Name the addition property shown: $27 + 0 = 27$. _____

9. Round the number 3.789 to the nearest tenth. _____

10. Stacey gave 4 pencils to each of 6 friends. How many pencils did she give away to her friends?

_____

11. Melba had 4 choices for snacks and 3 choices for drinks. How many different combinations of snacks and drinks could she have?

_____

Write and Evaluate Expressions

Write an expression. If you use a variable, tell what it represents.

1. Zachary has 3 cases filled with CDs. Each case holds 24 CDs.

_____

2. Janet was babysitting 3 children at the playground and 4 more came.

_____

3. Mrs. Smith canned 20 jars of peaches each day from Monday through Friday.

_____

4. The boys ate some cookies on Monday and 6 more on Tuesday.

_____

5. Alicia scored 3 goals in each soccer game. There were several soccer games.

_____

6. Bobbie had 24 pencils. He gave each of his five friends the same amount.

_____

7. Jackie made several necklaces. She put 7 beads on each necklace.

_____

8. The grocer put 12 cans on each shelf. There were 6 shelves.

_____

9. Kerry had many baseball cards. He gave each of his 3 friends 8 cards.

_____

Let $n = 7$. Write $<$, $>$, or $=$ in each $\bigcirc$.

10. $5 \times n \bigcirc 25 + 6$

11. $20 \times n \bigcirc 4 \times 5 \times n$

12. $n \times 6 \bigcirc 6 + n$

13. $n \times 8 \bigcirc (12 + n) \times 3$

14. $3 \times n \times 2 \bigcirc 6 \times n$

15. $(2 \times n) + 18 \bigcirc 4 \times 9$

Mixed Review

16. $\begin{array}{r} 341,811 \\ + 148,756 \\ \hline \end{array}$

17. $\begin{array}{r} 61,507 \\ - 28,147 \\ \hline \end{array}$

18. $\begin{array}{r} 34.81 \\ + 20.09 \\ \hline \end{array}$

19. $\begin{array}{r} 12.09 \\ - 7.46 \\ \hline \end{array}$

20. $7 \times 4 = n$ _____

21. $12 \times 5 = n$ _____

22. $9 \times 7 = n$ _____

Order of Operations

Vocabulary

Complete.

1. A set of rules used to evaluate expressions with more

   than one operation is the _____.

Evaluate the expression.

2. $4 + (2 \times 6) - 10$

3. $13 - 8 \div (2 \times 2)$

4. $20 \div 4 \times (13 - 5)$

_____   _____   _____

5. $(9 \times 3) + 3 \div 1$

6. $3 \times 5 + 8 - 4$

7. $30 \div (7 + 3) \times 8$

_____   _____   _____

Write *correct* if the order of operations is correct.
Otherwise, give the correct sequence of operations.

8. $6 \times 4 + 3 \div 3$ Multiply, add, and then divide.

_____

9. $15 \div (4 - 1) \times 7$ Subtract, divide, and then multiply.

_____

10. $7 + (8 + 5) \div 5$ Add, add, and then divide.

_____

For 11–12, rewrite the expression using parentheses to get
the given value for a, b, and c.

11. $28 - 3 \times 3 + 4$ **a.** 23   **b.** 79   **c.** 7

_____   _____   _____

12. $30 \div 5 \times 3 + 1$ **a.** 24   **b.** 19   **c.** 3

_____   _____   _____

Mixed Review

Round each number to the place of the underlined digit.

13. 8.$\underline{4}$32   14. 16.7$\underline{3}$9   15. 34.62$\underline{1}$5   16. 9.$\underline{1}$84   17. 26.7$\underline{5}$6

_____ _____ _____ _____ _____

Functions

Vocabulary

1. A relationship between two variables in which one

   quantity depends on the other is a _____.

Complete the function table.

2. $h = 7g$

g	5	6	7	8	9
h					

3. $b = 11a$

a	2	3	4	5	6
b					

4. $d = 9c - 6$

c	9	8	7	6	5
d					

5. $k = 6j + 12$

j	0	2	4	6	8
k					

6. $t = 125 - 10s$

s	10	8	6	4	2
t					

7. $v = 20 + 3u$

u	12	9	6	3	0
v					

8. $f = 45 - 4e + 1$

e	1	3	6	8	9
f					

9. $r = 70 + 6q - 8$

q	8	7	5	3	2
r					

Use the function. Find the output, *y* for each input, *x*.

10. $y = 26 - 4x + 2$ for $x = 0, 3, 6$

11. $y = 2x + 6$ for $x = 10, 12, 14$

_____   _____

Mixed Review

Find the sum or difference. Estimate to check.

12.
$$\begin{array}{r} 3.27 \\ 4.063 \\ + 7.941 \\ \hline \end{array}$$

13.
$$\begin{array}{r} 8.04 \\ - 2.53 \\ \hline \end{array}$$

14.
$$\begin{array}{r} 17.1 \\ - 6.075 \\ \hline \end{array}$$

15.
$$\begin{array}{r} 5.003 \\ 1.964 \\ + 12.37 \\ \hline \end{array}$$

16.
$$\begin{array}{r} 26.03 \\ - 8.8 \\ \hline \end{array}$$

17. Order 6.021, 6.201, 6.102, and 6.210 from *least* to *greatest*.

18. Order 0.9403, 0.439, 0.493, and 0.394 from *greatest* to *least*.

_____   _____

Problem Solving Strategy

Write an Equation

Write and solve an equation for each problem. Explain what the variable represents.

1. Mary ordered 4 chicken salads to take home for dinner. Her total bill came to $24. How much was each salad?

_____

_____

2. Marcus ran the same number of miles every day for ten days. He ran a total of 120 miles. How many miles did Marcus run each day?

_____

_____

3. Steve completed some homework papers on Monday. On Tuesday he finished 6 papers, twice what he did on Monday. How many did he do on Monday?

_____

_____

4. Martin rode his bicycle for a total of 140 miles. It took him 7 hours. If he rode the same number of miles each hour, how many miles did he travel every hour?

_____

_____

Mixed Review

5. $\begin{array}{r} 27 \\ -\ 9 \\ \hline \end{array}$

6. $\begin{array}{r} 43 \\ -\ 16 \\ \hline \end{array}$

7. $\begin{array}{r} 62 \\ -\ 8 \\ \hline \end{array}$

8. $\begin{array}{r} 91 \\ -\ 22 \\ \hline \end{array}$

9. $\begin{array}{r} 70 \\ -\ 11 \\ \hline \end{array}$

10. Two numbers have a difference of 10 and the sum of 34. What are the numbers?

_____

11. Dallas Fort Worth Airport had 678,492 passengers this year. Dallas Fort Worth had 26,239 more passengers than O'Hare. How many passengers did O'Hare airport have?

_____

Use Multiplication Properties

Solve the equation. Identify the property used.

1. $17 \times a = 23 \times 17$

_____

2. $(4 \times 2) \times 5 = 4 \times (p \times 5)$

_____

3. $n \times 1 = 240$

_____

4. $340 \times b = 0$

_____

5. $112 \times 13 = n \times 112$

_____

6. $8 \times (y \times 31) = (8 \times 7) \times 31$

_____

7. $71 \times k = 71$

_____

8. $(z \times 14) \times 8 = 9 \times (14 \times 8)$

_____

9. $65 \times 0 = h$

_____

10. $28 \times 6 = 6 \times c$

_____

Identify the property shown.

11. $16 \times p = 16$

_____

12. $(y \times p) \times t = y \times (p \times t)$

_____

13. $r \times s = s \times r$

_____

14. $b \times 0 = 0$

_____

Mixed Review

15. $\begin{array}{r} 4.482 \\ + 6.157 \\ \hline \end{array}$

16. $\begin{array}{r} 18.2546 \\ - 8.6207 \\ \hline \end{array}$

17. $\begin{array}{r} 159{,}402 \\ - 61{,}089 \\ \hline \end{array}$

18. $\begin{array}{r} 618{,}816 \\ + 372{,}452 \\ \hline \end{array}$

_____ _____ _____ _____

Write *equivalent* or *not equivalent* to describe each pair of decimals.

19. 2.103 and 2.130

20. 6.04 and 6.040

21. 5.015 and 5.150

_____ _____ _____

The Distributive Property

Vocabulary

Fill in the blanks.

1. The _____ _____ allows
   you to break apart numbers to make them easier to multiply.

Use the grid below to find the product.

2. $10 \times 17 =$ 3. $15 \times 14 =$

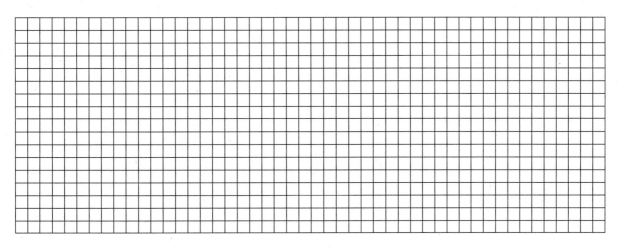

Use the Distributive Property to restate each expression. Find the product.

4. 12×18 5. 20×23 6. 30×33

_____   _____   _____

_____   _____   _____

_____   _____   _____

Restate the expression using the Distributive Property. Then find the value of the expression.

7. $6 \times (9 + n)$ if n is 30   8. $7 \times (n + 5)$ if n is 50   9. $n \times (8 + 60)$ if n is 3

_____   _____   _____

Mixed Review

Find the value of ■.

10. $7 + $ ■ $ = 4 + 32$ _____   11. ■ $ + 19 = 22 + 14$ _____

Collect and Organize Data

Vocabulary

1. The _____ is the difference between the greatest and least numbers in a set of data.

2. The _____ is a running total of the data that has been recorded.

For 3–6, use the frequency table.

3. How many fifth graders bought a pencil in Week 1?

    _____

    in Week 4?

    _____

4. By Week 3, how many fifth graders had bought a pencil?

    _____

FIFTH-GRADE PENCIL SALES		
Week	Frequency (Number of Pencils)	Cumulative Frequency
1	17	17
2	15	32
3	12	44
4	19	63

5. How many fifth graders bought pencils during the 4 weeks?

    _____

6. What is the range of the number of fifth graders who bought a pencil each week?

    _____

Find the range for each set of data.

7. 2, 5, 12, 7, 9

8. 63, 51, 67, 48, 56

9. 110, 121, 145, 116, 136

_____   _____   _____

Mixed Review

10. 17
    $\times 5$

11. 29
    $\times 6$

12. 44
    $\times 9$

13. 103
    $\times\ 7$

14. 422
    $\times\ 7$

Find the Mean

Vocabulary

1. The _____ of a group of numbers can be found by adding all of the data and then dividing by the number of addends.

2. Write the steps used to find the mean of a set of data.

   _____

Find the mean for each set of data.

3. 2, 8, 3, 8, 4

   _____

4. 30, 10, 20, 10, 10

   _____

5. $5, $8, $9, $14

   _____

6. 2, 4, 4, 4, 6, 7, 8

   _____

7. 3, 8, 21, 22, 36

   _____

8. 52, 97, 101, 118

   _____

9. 115, 110, 120, 100, 100

   _____

10. 220, 180, 160, 200, 160

    _____

Use the given mean to find the missing number in each data set.

11. 12, ■, 17; mean: 14

    _____

12. 7, 8, 8, ■; mean: 8

    _____

13. 1, 1, 2, 4, 5, ■, 10, 10; mean: 5

    _____

14. 76, 77, 77, ■, 86, 88, 91; mean: 82

    _____

Mixed Review

15.   64,578.903
      + 1,722,354.3

16. $169,468.00
     −   73,294.00

17.   727.9648
     − 130.0070

Find the Median and Mode

Vocabulary

1. The _____ is the middle number when the data are arranged in order.

2. The _____ is the number or numbers that occurs most often in a set of data.

Find the median and the mode for each set of data.

3.

Julian's Test Scores							
Test	1	2	3	4	5	6	7
Score	86	98	98	85	87	92	89

_____

4.

Students' Heights					
Name	Rose	Sally	Hank	John	Raj
Inches	57	53	55	56	57

_____

5.

Baseball Card Collection					
Name	Sam	Jen	Tad	Phil	Li
Number	300	280	320	280	340

_____

6.

Magazines Sold							
Week	1	2	3	4	5	6	7
Number	180	150	175	160	225	190	225

_____

Mixed Review

7. $4\overline{)2,636}$ 8. $8\overline{)7,978}$ 9. $4\overline{)1,102}$ 10. $8\overline{)760}$

11. $\begin{array}{r} 27 \\ 31 \\ + 19 \\ \hline \end{array}$ 12. $\begin{array}{r} 34 \\ 99 \\ + 26 \\ \hline \end{array}$ 13. $\begin{array}{r} 18 \\ 19 \\ + 17 \\ \hline \end{array}$ 14. $\begin{array}{r} 58 \\ 20 \\ + 30 \\ \hline \end{array}$ 15. $\begin{array}{r} 82 \\ 69 \\ + 49 \\ \hline \end{array}$

Problem Solving Strategy
Make a Graph

Vocabulary

1. A _____ organizes data by place value.

Make a graph to solve.

2. During science class the students recorded the height of their plants in centimeters. The heights were: 10, 12, 12, 13, 15, 18, 20, 21, 24, 36, 36, 38, 40.
   a. Do the plants usually grow in the 10's, 20's, 30's, or 40's?

   _____

   b. What is the range of the data?

   c. What is the median?

   d. What is the mode?

   _____   _____   _____

3. Mrs. Hill's students are doing a project about their grandparents' lives. Part of the project is to record the ages of their grandparents. The students list the following ages: 51, 53, 55, 55, 60, 61, 63, 67, 73 75, 80.
   a. What is the mean of their grandparents' ages?

   _____

   b. What is the range of the data?

   c. What is the median?

   d. What is the mode?

   _____   _____   _____

Mixed Review

Find the mean.

4. 22, 23, 59, 61, 65 _____

5. 88, 88, 89, 91, 89 _____

Analyze Graphs

For 1–3, use the bar graph.

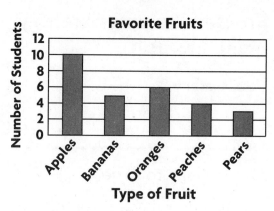

Favorite Fruits

1. Mark's class recorded their favorite fruits in a bar graph. Which type of fruit is most popular? How many students chose that fruit?

_____

2. How many more students chose apples than peaches?

_____

3. How many students recorded their favorite fruits?

_____

For 4–6, use the circle graph.

Steve's Monthly Entertainment Expenses

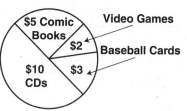

4. Steve made a circle graph to display his monthly expenses. What does Steve spend the least amount of money on each month? What does he spend the most on?

_____

5. On what two items does Steve spend about the same amount each month?

_____

6. How much does Steve spend in a month on comic books and baseball cards?

_____

Mixed Review

Solve.

7. $14 + n = 56$

_____

8. $27 - n = 1$

_____

Write in standard form.

9. seven and seven hundred twelve thousandths

_____

10. forty-one and three hundred eighty-seven ten-thousandths

_____

Name _____

Choose a Reasonable Scale

Vocabulary

Write the vocabulary word that best describes the part of a graph.

1. a series of numbers placed at fixed distances _____

2. the difference between one number and the
next on the scale _____

Choose a, b, c, or d as the most reasonable interval for the data.

3. 25, 50, 70, 75, 100   4. 2, 4, 1, 7, 5   a. 25

_____   _____   b. 5

5. 5, 10, 30, 40, 20   6. 15, 25, 35, 20, 40   c. 10

_____   _____   d. 1

Circle the letter of the more reasonable scale for the data.

7.

FIFTH-GRADE SURVEY	
Favorite Color	Number of Students
Red	40
Blue	50
Green	20
Yellow	10
Other	10

a. 60   b. 50
40   40
20   30
0   20
         10
         0

8.

CAKE SALE	
Week	Number Sold
1	10
2	5
3	15
4	12
5	20

a. 25   b. 80
20   60
15   40
10   20
5   0
0

Mixed Review

For 9–10, use the table.

9. What is a reasonable scale for the data?

_____

10. How many students were surveyed?

_____

SNACK SURVEY	
Favorite Snack	Number of Students
Oatmeal cookies	18
Sandwich	20
Fruit	10

Problem Solving Strategy
Make a Graph

Make a graph to solve.

1.

New Mascot		
Wolf	Bear	Lion
160	140	100

Mr. Brown, the principal, surveyed students to find out which mascot they wanted. He organized the data in a table. What graph should he use to display the data? What is a reasonable interval? scale? Make the graph.

_____

2.

Homework Pages Assigned					
Month	Sep	Oct	Nov	Dec	Jan
Number of Pages	40	60	80	40	80

Mr. Flores kept track of the number of homework pages assigned to the class for 5 months. He recorded the data in a table. What graph or plot should he use to display the data? What is a reasonable interval? scale? Make the graph.

_____

Mixed Review

3. Ben sold newspaper subscriptions. He sold 20 subscriptions on Monday and Tuesday, 15 subscriptions on Wednesday and Thursday, and 30 subscriptions on Friday. What is the mean number of subscriptions Ben sold?

_____

4. Samantha saved $35.50 to buy new clothes. She bought a shirt for $15.80 and a pair of pants for $12.75. How many pairs of socks priced at $1.99 a pair can she buy?

_____

5. The mean, median, and mode of 8, 5, 9, 6, 7, and ☐ are the same. What number is missing?

_____

6. Tracey has 4 coins in her pocket. If she has $0.46 in her pocket, what coins does she have?

_____

7. 49
× 6

8. 72
× 2

9. 34
× 8

10. 81
× 9

11. 57
× 8

Graph Ordered Pairs

Name the ordered pair for each point.

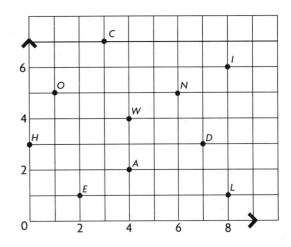

1. E _____

2. H _____

3. O _____

4. C _____

5. A _____

6. D _____

7. N _____

8. I _____

9. W _____

10. L _____

Graph and label the following points on a coordinate grid.

11. M (6, 1)   12. N (2, 5)   13. P (3, 4)   14. R (6, 3)

15. S (4, 6)   16. A (0, 5)   17. V (3, 7)   18. G (4, 1)

19. E (5, 0)   20. H (1, 7)   21. T (2, 6)   22. Y (1, 0)

Use the map for 23–25.

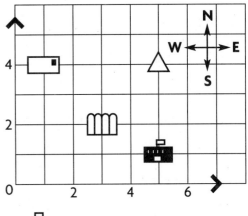

23. What direction would you go to go from the School to the City Hall?

_____

24. If each square represents one block, how many blocks is the Post Office from the Theater?

_____

25. Give directions to go from the School to the Post Office.

_____

 School    Post Office

Theater   △ City Hall

Mixed Review

26. Round 4,568,299 to the nearest 10,000.

27.   738,492
     − 586,238
     _____

28. What is the value of the underlined digit?

34,794,210

_____

_____

_____

Make Line Graphs

Vocabulary

Complete.

1. The _____ is the difference between the greatest and least numbers in a set of data.

Make a line graph for each set of data.

2.

Books Read					
Week	1	2	3	4	5
Number of Books	15	10	20	10	5

3.

Inches of Snowfall					
Month	Nov	Dec	Jan	Feb	Mar
Inches	4	12	8	6	2

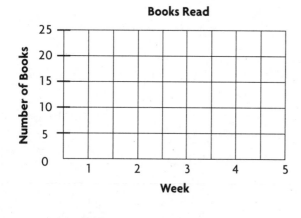

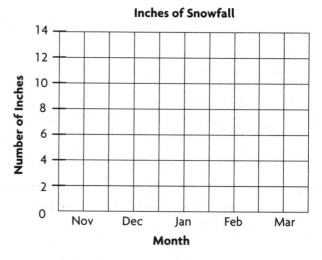

Mixed Review

For 4–5, use the table.

TIME SHEILA SPENDS PLAYING PIANO					
Day	Mon	Tue	Wed	Thu	Fri
Time	10 min	20 min	30 min	20 min	15 min

4. What would be a reasonable scale for a line graph displaying these data?

_____

5. What are the mean, median, and mode for the time Sheila spent playing the piano?

_____

Histograms

Vocabulary

Complete.

1. The _____ is a bar graph that shows the number of times data occur within intervals.

Decide which graph would better represent the data below, a bar graph or histogram. Then make each graph.

2.

Points Scored	Number of Players
21–25	13
26–30	16
31–35	12
36–40	8

3.

Favorite Month	Number of Students
December	42
June	38
August	29
July	31

_____

4.

Grade	Number of Students
First	104
Second	135
Third	124
Fourth	144
Fifth	122

5.

Heart Rate	Number of Students
54–57	4
58–61	12
62–65	14
66–69	18
70–73	25

_____

Mixed Review

6. $80,000 \times 6$

7. What is the value of the underlined digit?

249.5$\underline{6}$3

8. Write an equation to show the Property of One in multiplication.

_____

Choose the Appropriate Graph

For 1–4, choose the best type of graph or plot for the data.
Explain your choice.

1. monthly high temperatures for a city over a 6-month period

   _____

   _____

2. heights of students in a class

   _____

   _____

3. most popular athletic shoe brand in a class

   _____

   _____

4. money spent on food each week over a 5-week period

   _____

   _____

Draw the graph or plot that best displays each set of data.

5.

Money Earned For Trip					
Week	1	2	3	4	5
Amount	$50	$40	$60	$80	$90

6.

Favorite TV Network	ABZ	CAT	DOG	ROX	CAN
Sixth Graders	5	10	20	20	30
Third Graders	20	15	15	30	5

Mixed Review

For 7–8, use the table.

7. What type of graph would you use to display the data? Explain.

   _____

8. What number of pets do the most students own?

   _____

Pets Owned by Mr. Craig's Students						
Number of Pets	0	1	2	3	4	5
Number of Students	5	7	6	8	2	1

9. 493,487
   + 231,147

10. 946,493
    − 128,518

Estimation: Patterns in Multiples

Estimate each product.

1. 5 × 2,346

_____

2. 7 × 8,943

_____

3. 54 × 237

_____

4. 66 × 2,159

_____

5. 32 × 4,742

_____

6. 89 × 3,456

_____

7. 54 × 4,576

_____

8. 76 × 543

_____

9. 54 × 893

_____

10. 67 × 238

_____

11. 98 × 308

_____

12. 76 × 3,480

_____

13. 765 × 78

_____

14. 432 × 89

_____

15. 567 × 23

_____

Mixed Review

16. 78,322
    −66,328

17. 98,754
    +54,672

18. 309
    × 23

19. 715
    × 16

20. Write in word form: 23,571

_____

21. Write in expanded form: 4,321

_____

22. Round 26.9865 to the nearest thousandth. _____

23. Round 795.8716 to the nearest hundredth. _____

Name _____

Multiply by 1–Digit Numbers

Find each product. Estimate to check.

1. $\begin{array}{r} 7{,}618 \\ \times\qquad 8 \\ \hline \end{array}$

2. $\begin{array}{r} 9{,}853 \\ \times\qquad 6 \\ \hline \end{array}$

3. $\begin{array}{r} 43{,}702 \\ \times\qquad 5 \\ \hline \end{array}$

Write $<$, $>$, or $=$ in each $\bigcirc$.

4. $7{,}899 \times 4 \bigcirc 1{,}999 \times 9$

5. $44{,}333 \times 6 \bigcirc 88{,}321 \times 3$

6. $63{,}809 \times 2 \bigcirc 54{,}902 \times 8$

7. $56{,}790 \times 2 \bigcirc 28{,}395 \times 4$

For 8–11, use the table.

Item	Cost
Baseball	$5.95
Bat	$7.90
Hat	$9.20
Glove	$15.60

8. Max purchased 3 baseballs. How much did he spend?

9. Jake purchased 2 gloves and a hat. How much did he spend?

10. How much will Mr. Carrington spend to buy one of each item?

11. The team gave a glove to each of its 9 players. How much did it cost to provide the gloves?

Mixed Review

12. Solve the equation: $n + 7 = 15$ _____

13. Evaluate $n + 7 - (2 \times 6)$ when $n = 5$. _____

14. Find the median of 44, 47, 49, 54, 67. _____

15. Find the mode of 54, 67, 82, 54, 90. _____

16. Find the mean of 34, 25, 68, 45. _____

Name _____

Multiply by 2–Digit Numbers

Find each product. Estimate to check.

1. 24
    ×46

2. 16
    ×37

3. 43
    ×54

4. 74
    ×47

5. 246
    × 22

6. 137
    × 65

7. 758
    × 14

8. 420
    × 31

9. 2,474
    × 16

10. 3,245
     × 25

11. 4,080
     × 35

12. 1,625
     × 30

Write <, >, or = in each ◯.

13. 13 × 28 ◯ 25 × 14

14. 24 × 12 ◯ 16 × 18

15. 123 × 15 ◯ 124 × 16

16. 33 × 45 ◯ 45 × 33

17. 231 × 21 ◯ 213 × 31

18. 2,002 × 34 ◯ 2,020 × 23

Mixed Review

19. Seth, Brian, and Mark are comparing their heights. At 52 inches, Seth is 6 inches taller than Brian. Brian is 3 inches shorter than Mark. How tall is Mark?

20. Write five hundred two and three hundred nine thousandths in standard form.

_____

_____

21. 38
     × 6

22. 72
     × 5

23. 66
     × 9

24. 23
     × 3

25. 42
     × 8

Choose a Method

Find the product.

1. $408 \times 562 =$

_____

2. $329 \times 1,123 =$

_____

3. $2,147 \times 415 =$

_____

4. $336 \times 483 =$

_____

5. $212 \times 3,678 =$

_____

6. $4,552 \times 53 =$

_____

7. $\begin{array}{r} 1,216 \\ \times\ \ \ \ 15 \\ \hline \end{array}$

8. $\begin{array}{r} 1,714 \\ \times\ \ \ \ 49 \\ \hline \end{array}$

9. $\begin{array}{r} 2,431 \\ \times\ \ \ \ 76 \\ \hline \end{array}$

10. $\begin{array}{r} 3,239 \\ \times\ \ \ \ 64 \\ \hline \end{array}$

11. $\begin{array}{r} 4,256 \\ \times\ \ \ \ 39 \\ \hline \end{array}$

12. $\begin{array}{r} 6,274 \\ \times\ \ \ \ 95 \\ \hline \end{array}$

13. $\begin{array}{r} 1,495 \\ \times\ \ \ 627 \\ \hline \end{array}$

14. $\begin{array}{r} 2,501 \\ \times\ \ \ 251 \\ \hline \end{array}$

15. $\begin{array}{r} 6,328 \\ \times\ \ \ 346 \\ \hline \end{array}$

Mixed Review

Find the value of *n*.

16. $(36 \div n) \times 20 = 120$

17. $22 + (n - 4) = 79$

18. $38 + n + 68.5 = 149.80$

19. $\$12.42 \div (17 - n) = \$4.14$

20. Sophia ran the 100-meter dash in 11.36 seconds. What is the value of the 3 in her time?

21. Find the difference. Estimate to check.

$\begin{array}{r} 78,932 \\ -\ 65,345 \\ \hline \end{array}$

Problem Solving Skill

Evaluate Answers for Reasonableness

Write the most reasonable answer without solving.

1. Walter prints 234,897 magazines per day in his shop. He says he prints more than 6,000,000 magazines a month. Is his answer reasonable? Explain.

_____

_____

2. The car dealer in town purchased 478 cars, each one costing $19,453. He said he paid $929,534 for the cars. Is his answer reasonable?

_____

Choose the most reasonable answer without solving.

3. Eddie saves $5 per week for a bike. After three years approximately how much did he save?

A $15

B $25

C $500

D $750

4. A mayor received about 334,000 votes from each of 3 different areas. About how many votes did he receive?

F 100,000 votes

G 111,000 votes

H 1,000,000 votes

J 1,110,000 votes

Mixed Review

Use data from the graph to answer 5–7.

5. What was the approximate difference in numbers of male and female athletes during 1987?

_____

6. What was the approximate difference in numbers of male and female athletes during 1988?

_____

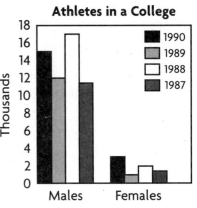

Athletes in a College

7. What was the approximate total number of athletes during 1989?

_____

Multiply Decimals and Whole Numbers

Make a model to find each product.

1. 2×0.5 **2.** 3×0.4 **3.** 2×0.25 **4.** 0.17×3

_____   _____   _____   _____

5. 4×0.7 **6.** 0.11×4 **7.** 3×0.8 **8.** 0.33×2

_____   _____   _____   _____

Phillip is buying school supplies at the student book store.
For 9–13, use the pictures to find the total cost.

9. 2 pencils, 2 erasers

_____

10. 2 markers, 1 protractor

_____

11. 3 pencils, 2 compasses

_____

12. 4 markers, 2 erasers, 1 protractor

_____

13. 3 compasses, 2 markers, 1 pencil

_____

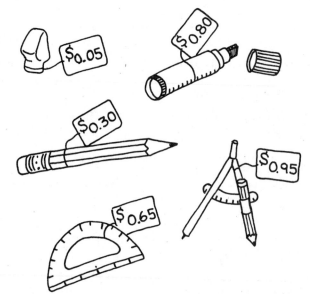

Mixed Review

14. Phyllis is shopping at the student bookstore. Which cost more— 2 markers, or 1 compass and 2 pencils?

_____

15. Sam has $0.36. He has 5 coins. What are they?

_____

16. 335,657 $\times$ 8

17. 7,612 $\times$ 15

18. 101,483 $\times$ 50

19. 492,655 $\times$ 17

Algebra: Patterns in Decimal Factors and Products

Use mental math to complete.

1. $1 \times 0.007 = 0.007$
$10 \times 0.007 = 0.07$
$100 \times 0.007 = 0.7$
$1{,}000 \times 0.007 = \square$

_____

2. $1 \times 0.034 = 0.034$
$10 \times 0.034 = 0.34$
$100 \times 0.034 = \square$
$1{,}000 \times 0.034 = 34$

_____

3. $1 \times 0.0061 = 0.0061$
$10 \times 0.0061 = \square$
$100 \times 0.0061 = 0.61$
$1{,}000 \times 0.0061 = \square$

_____

4. $1 \times 0.53 = 0.53$
$10 \times 0.53 = \square$
$100 \times 0.53 = \square$
$1{,}000 \times 0.53 = 530$

_____

5. $1 \times 0.0817 = 0.0817$
$10 \times 0.0817 = \square$
$100 \times 0.0817 = \square$
$1{,}000 \times 0.0817 = \square$

_____

6. $1 \times 0.49 = 0.49$
$10 \times 0.49 = \square$
$100 \times 0.49 = \square$
$1{,}000 \times 0.49 = \square$

_____

Multiply each number by 10, by 100, and by 1,000.

7. 0.4

_____

8. 0.16

_____

9. 0.7832

_____

10. $0.17

_____

11. $1.19

_____

12. 5.9173

_____

Find the value of *n*.

13. $10 \times n = 8$

_____

14. $100 \times 0.625 = n$

_____

15. $n \times 100 = 0.7$

_____

16. $1{,}000 \times 0.23 = n$

_____

17. $100 \times n = 50$

_____

18. $10 \times n = 50.3$

_____

Mixed Review

19. What is the place value of the digit 6 in the number 162,083?

_____

20. Which digits make
11. $\square$57 < 11.407 true?

_____

Name _____

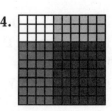

LESSON 10.3

Model Decimal Multiplication

Complete the multiplication sentence for each model.

1.  2. 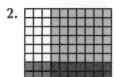 3. 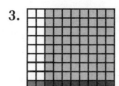 4.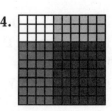

$0.3 \times 0.4 = n$ $n \times 0.7 = 0.28$ $n \times 0.8 = 0.16$ $0.7 \times n = 0.42$

_____   _____   _____   _____

Make a model to find the product.

5. 0.4×0.6 **6.** 0.1×0.5 **7.** 0.8×0.3 **8.** 0.6×0.9

_____   _____   _____   _____

Find the product.

9. 0.7×0.6 _____   **10.** 0.4×0.9 _____   **11.** 0.9×0.3 _____

12. 0.8×0.6 _____   **13.** 0.2×0.5 _____   **14.** 0.5×0.3 _____

15. 0.8×0.5 _____   **16.** 0.1×0.9 _____   **17.** 0.4×0.4 _____

18. 0.7×0.5 _____   **19.** 0.2×0.6 _____   **20.** 0.6×0.6 _____

21. 0.5×0.4 _____   **22.** 0.8×0.7 _____   **23.** 0.9×0.5 _____

24. 0.6×0.3 _____   **25.** 0.4×0.2 _____   **26.** 0.7×0.7 _____

Find the value of *n*.

27. $n \times 0.3 = 0.15$ **28.** $0.7 \times n = 0.56$ **29.** $n \times 0.6 = 0.36$ **30.** $0.9 \times n = 0.36$

_____   _____   _____   _____

Mixed Review

31. $3.6 + 4.3$ **32.** $7.6 + 0.75$ **33.** $16.3 + 0.07$ **34.** $6.3 + 1.48$

_____   _____   _____   _____

Place the Decimal Point

Choose the best estimate. Write *a*, *b*, or *c*.

1. 11×0.3

    a. 3   **b.** 30   **c.** 300

_____

2. 24×0.6

    a. 1.2   **b.** 12   **c.** 120

_____

3. 42×0.9

    a. 4   **b.** 40   **c.** 400

_____

4. 36×0.4

    a. 0.9   **b.** 6   **c.** 15

_____

5. $\$0.83 \times 2$

    a. $1.60   **b.** $16.00   **c.** $160.00

_____

6. $\$0.43 \times 5$

    a. $0.20   **b.** $2.00   **c.** $4.00

_____

Find the product. Estimate to check.

7. 0.5×28 **8.** 2.6×3.9 **9.** 0.72×317 **10.** 5.64×9.7

_____

Find the product.

11. 0.2×0.6 **12.** 1.2×0.7 **13.** 0.83×0.29 **14.** 9.1×3.7

_____

Copy the answer. Place the decimal point in the product.

15.   7.2
     $\times \ 4$
     288

16.   0.58
     $\times \ 7$
     406

17.   4.218
     $\times \ 0.31$
     130758

18.   2.723
     $\times \ 8.149$
     22189727

_____

Mixed Review

19. What is the range of the data 12, 33, 19, 79, 44, 48?

20. Evaluate $(n \times 6) \times 4$ if $n = 2$.

21. Write five ten thousandths as a decimal.

_____

Name _____

Zeros in the Product

Find the product.

1. 2 × 0.04   **2.** 9 × 0.007   **3.** 0.6 × 0.07   **4.** 43.1 × 0.03

_____   _____   _____   _____

5. 0.008   **6.** 0.07   **7.** 0.004   **8.** 0.065
  × 7   × 7   × 13.7   × 0.09

9. 93.27   **10.** 0.0042   **11.** 0.0061   **12.** 0.008
  × 0.03   × 78   × 0.5   × 0.05

Find the product. Round to the nearest cent.

13. $0.34 × 0.09   **14.** $7.18 × 0.03   **15.** $0.92 × 0.08   **16.** $73.62 × 0.06

_____   _____   _____   _____

Write <, >, or = for each ◯.

17. 0.03 × 0.09 ◯ 0.3 × 0.009   **18.** 0.07 × 0.4 ◯ 0.007 × 0.4

_____   _____

19. 0.45 × 0.01 ◯ 0.005 × 0.91   **20.** 0.076 × 0.8 ◯ 0.08 × 0.76

_____   _____

Mixed Review

21.   13,788   **22.**   77.028   **23.** 150.257   **24.**   563,072
      + 43,791   + 12.937   − 73.084   + 337,944

25. 5,073   **26.** $194.20   **27.** 91.836   **28.** $421.99
    + 312   + $31.57   − 12.900   + $87.02

Name _____

Problem Solving Skill:
Make Decisions

For 1–4, use the information in the table.

Item	Store A	Store B	Store C
Cheese	$0.49	$0.33	$0.59
Peppers	$0.99	$1.05	$1.09
Sausage	$2.59	$2.10	$1.99
Pepperoni	$2.69	$2.30	$2.90

You are planning to make a pizza. You want one of each of the items in the table above.

1. If you could go to only one store to buy all of the items, to which store would you go? Why?

2. If you could go to more than one store, what is the least you could spend?

3. If you could go to only stores A and B or stores B and C, what is the least you could spend? What stores would you go to?

4. It costs $1.23 to drive to store A, $2.44 to drive to store B, and $1.30 to drive to store C. You can go to only one store. To which store would you go now? What is the total cost?

Mixed Review

Multiply each number by 10, by 100, and by 1,000.

5. 0.6

6. 7.2

7. 0.0012

8. 0.043

Find the value of n.

9. $1,024 - 718 = n$

10. $100 \times 0.4 = n$

11. $n \times 1,000 = 0.6$

Name _____

Estimate Quotients

Vocabulary

Fill in the blanks.

1. _____ are numbers
   that are easy to compute mentally.

Estimate the quotient. Tell what compatible numbers you used.

2. $817 \div 4$ 3. $462 \div 9$ 4. $703 \div 7$ 5. $492 \div 8$

   _____   _____   _____   _____

6. $281 \div 3$ 7. $5,391 \div 6$ 8. $29,537 \div 3$ 9. $293,765 \div 5$

   _____   _____   _____   _____

Estimate the quotient, using two sets of compatible numbers.

10. $3\overline{)144}$ 11. $6\overline{)1,745}$ 12. $9\overline{)1,538}$ 13. $7\overline{)47,676}$

14. $2\overline{)24,918}$ 15. $4\overline{)85,576}$ 16. $7\overline{)799,321}$ 17. $8\overline{)385,678}$

Mixed Review

18. $25,294$ 19. $193,867$ 20. 3.67 21. 9.28 22. $72,014$
    $\times\quad 38$ $\times\quad 45$ $\times 0.05$ $\times 0.14$ $+ 36,958$

23. $7\overline{)69}$ 24. $4\overline{)83}$ 25. $5\overline{)73}$ 26. $8\overline{)36}$ 27. $4\overline{)95}$

Name _____

Divide 3-Digit Dividends

Name the position of the first digit of the quotient.

1. $4\overline{)832}$ 2. $2\overline{)417}$ 3. $7\overline{)217}$ 4. $6\overline{)213}$

_____ _____ _____ _____

Divide.

5. $9\overline{)326}$ 6. $3\overline{)235}$ 7. $6\overline{)367}$ 8. $4\overline{)935}$

9. $6\overline{)115}$ 10. $9\overline{)504}$ 11. $7\overline{)219}$ 12. $5\overline{)621}$

Find the value of n.

13. $517 \div 2 = n$ 14. $n \div 3 = 203$ 15. $785 \div n = 112\,r1$ 16. $431 \div 6 = n$

_____ _____ _____ _____

17. On Friday and Saturday, 618 people attended a car show. If the same number of people went each day, how many people attended the car show on Saturday?

18. Sue drove 364 miles in 7 hours. How many miles did she drive in 1 hour?

Mixed Review

19. $\begin{array}{r} 5,862 \\ + 6,374 \\ \hline \end{array}$

20. $\begin{array}{r} 93,042 \\ - 54,878 \\ \hline \end{array}$

21. $\begin{array}{r} 29,038 \\ \times \quad 72 \\ \hline \end{array}$

22. $\begin{array}{r} 153,911 \\ - 68,099 \\ \hline \end{array}$

23. $\begin{array}{r} 49,499 \\ \times \quad 5 \\ \hline \end{array}$

24. $\begin{array}{r} 61,711 \\ - 30,490 \\ \hline \end{array}$

25. $\begin{array}{r} 9,715 \\ + 2,243 \\ \hline \end{array}$

26. $\begin{array}{r} 22,675 \\ \times \quad 30 \\ \hline \end{array}$

Zeros in Division

Divide. Estimate to check.

1. $8\overline{)330}$ 2. $6\overline{)371}$ 3. $2\overline{)813}$ 4. $9\overline{)625}$

5. $5\overline{)535}$ 6. $3\overline{)924}$ 7. $4\overline{)836}$ 8. $6\overline{)615}$

9. $2\overline{)610}$ 10. $9\overline{)960}$ 11. $7\overline{)423}$ 12. $8\overline{)647}$

Find the value of n.

13. $902 \div 9 = n$ 14. $n \div 2 = 204 \text{ r1}$ 15. $142 \div n = 28 \text{ r2}$ 16. $821 \div 8 = n$

_____   _____   _____   _____

17. On Saturday and Sunday, a total of 908 people visited the museum. If the same number of people came each day, how many went to the museum on Sunday?

18. During a 5-hour period, 510 lunches were sold in a cafeteria. If the same number of lunches were sold each hour, how many lunches were sold during the first hour?

_____   _____

Mixed Review

19. $\begin{array}{r} 1.75 \\ + 4.93 \\ \hline \end{array}$

20. $\begin{array}{r} 2.34 \\ \times 0.31 \\ \hline \end{array}$

21. $\begin{array}{r} 48 \\ \times 84 \\ \hline \end{array}$

22. $\begin{array}{r} 2,476,935 \\ + 3,983,566 \\ \hline \end{array}$

23. $\begin{array}{r} 72 \\ \times 27 \\ \hline \end{array}$

24. $\begin{array}{r} 6,505 \\ \times \quad 2 \\ \hline \end{array}$

25. $\begin{array}{r} 4.28 \\ - 3.79 \\ \hline \end{array}$

26. $\begin{array}{r} 52 \\ \times 80 \\ \hline \end{array}$

27. $\begin{array}{r} 6,721,400 \\ - 4,055,981 \\ \hline \end{array}$

28. $\begin{array}{r} 33 \\ \times 56 \\ \hline \end{array}$

Choose a Method

Divide.

1. $5\overline{)5,379}$ 2. $7\overline{)3,942}$ 3. $4\overline{)8,632}$ 4. $4\overline{)2,434}$

5. $7\overline{)6,015}$ 6. $2\overline{)19,673}$ 7. $8\overline{)34,763}$ 8. $9\overline{)52,845}$

9. $48,592 \div 8$ 10. $78,787 \div 3$ 11. $81,438 \div 6$ 12. $99,228 \div 9$

_____   _____   _____   _____

13. $45,980 \div 2$ 14. $299,344 \div 7$ 15. $752,638 \div 8$ 16. $430,572 \div 2$

_____   _____   _____   _____

Mixed Review

17. Write the place value of the **bold-faced** digit: 4,5**3**2,703,689

18. Write the standard form for one billion, thirty-four million, five hundred thousand, nine hundred eighty-two.

19. Order from greatest to least: 63,545; 63,454; 64,455; 64,544.

_____   _____   _____

20.   97,036
    − 53,987

21.   635,837
    + 283,496

22.   853,969
    ×   17

23.   38.72
    − 17.09

Name _____

Algebra: Expressions and Equations

Evaluate the expression $2,460 \div n$ for each value of n.

1. $n = 6$ **2.** $n = 3$ **3.** $n = 2$ **4.** $n = 5$

_____ _____ _____ _____

Evaluate the expression for each value of n.

5. $n \div 6$
$n = 54, 96, 138$

_____

6. $216 \div n$
$n = 3, 4, 9$

_____

7. $n \div 8$
$n = 64, 256, 328$

_____

8. $4,832 \div n$
$n = 2, 4, 8$

_____

Determine which value is a solution for the given equation.

9. $54 \div n = 6$
$n = 3, 6$ or 9

10. $136 \div n = 34$
$n = 6, 2$ or 4

11. $n \div 5 = 42$
$n = 200$ or 210

12. $265 \div n = 5$
$n = 51$ or 53

_____ _____ _____ _____

Solve the equation. Then check the solution.

13. $45 \div n = 9$ **14.** $32 \div n = 4$ **15.** $48 \div n = 12$ **16.** $n \div 8 = 9$

_____ _____ _____ _____

Mixed Review

17. 23.74
$+ 0.25$

18. 23.74
$\times 0.25$

19. 2.48
$\times 0.77$

20. 39.60
$- 25.72$

21. 59.61
$\times 0.15$

Name _____

Problem Solving Skill

Interpret the Remainder

Solve and then explain how you interpreted the remainder.

1. A total of 124 players were riding a bus to the soccer game. If 25 players can ride in each bus, how many buses are needed?

2. There are 230 books in the storeroom. Each box holds 33 books. How many boxes are needed to store all of the books?

3. Lauren's piece of wire is 5 times as long as Larry's wire. Lauren's wire is 8 cm long. How long is Larry's wire?

4. Lee's Bakery sells muffins by the dozen. The bakery has 230 muffins prepared. Does the bakery have enough muffins to fill 20 orders?

5. Sue has 85 flowers. She put them in 7 vases with the same number of flowers in each vase except one. How many flowers are in the vase with the greatest number of flowers?

6. Jeremy had 75 feet of string. He divided it into 4 equal pieces. How long was each piece of string?

Mixed Review

7. $\begin{array}{r} 5,232 \\ -\ 2,989 \end{array}$

8. $\begin{array}{r} 9.71 \\ \times\ 0.36 \end{array}$

9. $\begin{array}{r} 7.043 \\ \times\ 0.620 \end{array}$

10. $\begin{array}{r} 455 \\ \times\ 23 \end{array}$

11. $\begin{array}{r} 7.790 \\ \times\ 0.431 \end{array}$

12. $121 \div 11 =$ _____

13. $96 \div 12 =$ _____

14. $108 \div 12 =$ _____

Name _____

Algebra: Patterns in Division

Use mental math to complete. Write the basic fact you use.

1. $100 \div 2 =$ ___
   $1,000 \div 2 = 500$
   $10,000 \div 2 = 5,000$

2. $900 \div 90 = 10$
   $9,000 \div 90 =$ ___
   $90,000 \div 90 = 1,000$

3. $300 \div 50 = 6$
   $3,000 \div 50 = 60$
   $30,000 \div 50 =$ ___

4. $140 \div 20 = 7$
   $1,400 \div 20 =$ ___
   $14,000 \div 20 = 700$

5. $250 \div 50 =$ ___
   $2,500 \div 50 = 50$
   $25,000 \div 50 = 500$

6. $360 \div 60 = 6$
   $3,600 \div 60 = 60$
   $36,000 \div 60 =$ ___

Use basic facts and patterns to solve for n.

7. $120 \div 4 = n$

8. $320 \div 80 = n$

9. $810 \div 90 = n$

10. $350 \div 70 = n$

11. $480 \div 60 = n$

12. $720 \div n = 9$

13. $4,000 \div 80 = n$

14. $2,000 \div n = 100$

15. $5,400 \div n = 90$

16. $3,600 \div n = 90$

17. $5,600 \div n = 800$

18. $2,700 \div n = 30$

Compare. Use $<$, $>$, or $=$ in each $\bigcirc$.

19. $24,000 \div 80 \bigcirc 2,400 \div 800$

20. $1,200 \div 3 \bigcirc 12,000 \div 30$

21. $54,000 \div 600 \bigcirc 540 \div 60$

22. $14,000 \div 70 \bigcirc 140 \div 7$

Mixed Review

23. $758,204$
    $+675,938$

24. 19.654
    $- 3.789$

25. 20.03
    $\times 0.56$

26. $672 \div 9$ ___

Name _____

Estimate Quotients

Write two pairs of compatible numbers for each. Give two
possible estimates.

1. $359 \div 55 = n$

2. $715 \div 74 = n$

3. $156 \div 37 = n$

_____

_____

4. $438 \div 57 = n$

5. $1,893 \div 52 = n$

6. $3,127 \div 44 = n$

_____

_____

Estimate the quotient.

7. $18\overline{)175}$ **8.** $37\overline{)231}$ **9.** $62\overline{)375}$ **10.** $81\overline{)255}$

11. $53\overline{)2,681}$ **12.** $41\overline{)3,289}$ **13.** $79\overline{)4,007}$ **14.** $29\overline{)1,811}$

15. $34\overline{)241}$ **16.** $53\overline{)4,787}$ **17.** $47\overline{)388}$ **18.** $68\overline{)3,594}$

Name the compatible numbers used to find the estimate.

19. $725 \div 19$
estimate: 35

20. $3,641 \div 34$
estimate: 120

21. $2,913 \div 72$
estimate: 40

22. $439 \div 44$
estimate: 10

_____

Mixed Review

23. 345
$\times\ 89$

24. $4,578,459$
$+7,612,501$

25. $54,607$
$-23,999$

26. $10\overline{)4,000}$

27. $366,546$
$+601,593$

28. $614,760$
$-407,345$

29. 908
$\times\ 57$

30. $10\overline{)9,650}$

Divide by 2-Digit Divisors

Name the position of the first digit of the quotient.

1. $17\overline{)1,527}$ **2.** $23\overline{)1,941}$ **3.** $34\overline{)7,109}$ **4.** $45\overline{)5,683}$

_____   _____   _____   _____

5. $89\overline{)9,266}$ **6.** $31\overline{)6,683}$ **7.** $24\overline{)1,742}$ **8.** $87\overline{)9,556}$

_____   _____   _____   _____

Divide. Check by multiplying.

9. $433 \div 35$ **10.** $698 \div 22$ **11.** $582 \div 41$ **12.** $3,121 \div 81$

_____   _____   _____   _____

13. $7,506 \div 64$ **14.** $8,921 \div 59$ **15.** $21,472 \div 75$ **16.** $14,117 \div 17$

_____   _____   _____   _____

Divide.

17. $72\overline{)8,136}$ **18.** $39\overline{)4,579}$ **19.** $27\overline{)2,835}$ **20.** $49\overline{)7,116}$

21. $13\overline{)3,926}$ **22.** $81\overline{)9,446}$ **23.** $35\overline{)7,105}$ **24.** $6\overline{)3,109}$

Match each check with a division problem.

25. $(43 \times 21) + 10 = 913$ _____   **a.** $10,738 \div 76 = 141 \text{ r}22$

26. $(76 \times 141) + 22 = 10,738$ _____   **b.** $6,348 \div 51 = 124 \text{ r}24$

27. $(28 \times 152) + 4 = 4,260$ _____   **c.** $913 \div 43 = 21 \text{ r}10$

28. $(51 \times 124) + 24 = 6,348$ _____   **d.** $4,260 \div 28 = 152 \text{ r}4$

Mixed Review

29. $\begin{array}{r} 35,482 \\ +28,453 \end{array}$ **30.** $\begin{array}{r} 6.75 \\ \times 0.75 \end{array}$ **31.** $\begin{array}{r} 92.99 \\ +\ 36.87 \end{array}$ **32.** $\begin{array}{r} 123 \\ \times 98 \end{array}$ **33.** $\begin{array}{r} 42,000 \\ +\ 1,212 \end{array}$

Correcting Quotients

Write *too high*, *too low*, or *just right* for each estimate.

1. $\overset{2}{34\overline{)105}}$

2. $\overset{5}{17\overline{)89}}$

3. $\overset{8}{42\overline{)295}}$

4. $\overset{5}{23\overline{)119}}$

_____ _____ _____ _____

5. $\overset{90}{26\overline{)2,350}}$

6. $\overset{90}{36\overline{)2,917}}$

7. $\overset{300}{91\overline{)19,563}}$

8. $\overset{400}{56\overline{)32,762}}$

_____ _____ _____ _____

Choose the better estimate to use for the quotient. Circle *a* or *b*.

9. $23\overline{)94}$ **a.** 4   **b.** 5

10. $41\overline{)173}$ **a.** 3   **b.** 4

11. $68\overline{)5,720}$ **a.** 70   **b.** 80

12. $58\overline{)31,167}$ **a.** 400   **b.** 600

Divide.

13. $76\overline{)308}$

14. $23\overline{)711}$

15. $14\overline{)296}$

16. $39\overline{)177}$

17. $46\overline{)1,726}$

18. $29\overline{)544}$

19. $13\overline{)98,603}$

20. $57\overline{)3,826}$

Mixed Review

21. A total of 635 people signed up for a bus trip. Each bus can hold 48 people. Will 13 buses be enough for the trip?

22. The bakery can make 15 apple pies and 8 blueberry pies every hour. How many pies can the bakery produce in 16 hours?

_____ _____

23. $20\overline{)4,000}$

24. $\begin{array}{r} 417,389 \\ +\quad 2,560 \\ \hline \end{array}$

25. $\begin{array}{r} 6,243 \\ -4,709 \\ \hline \end{array}$

26. $\begin{array}{r} 12.5 \\ \times 0.6 \\ \hline \end{array}$

Practice Division

Divide.

1. $16\overline{)73}$ 2. $37\overline{)850}$ 3. $55\overline{)926}$ 4. $79\overline{)3,177}$

5. $35\overline{)219}$ 6. $96\overline{)7,428}$ 7. $41\overline{)2,659}$ 8. $27\overline{)1,167}$

9. $71\overline{)60,368}$ 10. $54\overline{)44,978}$ 11. $22\overline{)39,161}$ 12. $67\overline{)46,514}$

13. $63\overline{)4,144}$ 14. $37\overline{)2,187}$ 15. $84\overline{)76,167}$ 16. $52\overline{)78,667}$

17. $4,581 \div 32$ 18. $1,985 \div 23$ 19. $8,042 \div 91$

_____   _____   _____

20. $25,401 \div 25$ 21. $11,933 \div 42$ 22. $3,751 \div 55$

_____   _____   _____

Mixed Review

23. The students at Walnut Street School collected 3,102 cans for a recycling center. Each student brought in 6 cans. How many students attend the school?

_____

24. The Sweet Shoppe sold 2,610 ice cream cones during the 30 days of June. It sold the same number of cones each day. How many cones were sold per day?

_____

25. 87.562
    -14.787

26. 25.76
    $+68.34$

27. 8.09
    $\times 0.35$

28. $25\overline{)800}$

Problem Solving Strategy

Predict and Test

Predict and test to solve.

1. Scott is 5 years old. His Aunt Mary is 4 times as old. In how many years will Scott be half as old as his aunt will be at that time?

_____

2. The sum of two numbers is 42. Their product is 360. What are the two numbers?

_____

3. A tunnel toll is $1.25 for cars and $2.00 for trucks. In one hour, $40.00 is collected from 23 vehicles. How many cars and trucks paid the toll?

_____

4. Bob has 276 baseball cards. He keeps them in equal groups in boxes, and has started a new box with 3 cards in it. How many boxes of cards does he have? How many baseball cards are in each box?

_____

Mixed Review

Solve.

5. 92,074
    ×   18

6. 36,415
    ×   39

7. 70,851
    ×   42

8. 608,717
    ×   17

9. 9)2,304

10. 7)5,635

11. 4)9,004

12. 6)5,952

13. The Scouts washed 12 cars one afternoon. They earned $6.50 for each car they washed. How much money did they earn?

_____

14. What is 12.0143 rounded to the nearest hundredth?

Name _____

Algebra: Patterns in Decimal Division

Complete each pattern.

1. $600 \div 4 =$ _____

   $60 \div 4 =$ _____

   $6 \div 4 =$ _____

2. $100 \div 5 =$ _____

   $10 \div 5 =$ _____

   $1 \div 5 =$ _____

3. $200 \div 5 =$ _____

   $20 \div 5 =$ _____

   $2 \div 5 =$ _____

4. $100 \div 4 =$ _____

   $10 \div 4 =$ _____

   $1 \div 4 =$ _____

5. $1,400 \div 5 =$ _____

   $140 \div 5 =$ _____

   $14 \div 5 =$ _____

6. $1,000 \div 4 =$ _____

   $100 \div 4 =$ _____

   $10 \div 4 =$ _____

Complete each table. Use patterns and mental math.

7.

n	$n \div 20$
10,000	_____
1,000	_____
100	_____
10	_____

8.

n	$n \div 90$
36,000	_____
_____	40
_____	4
36	_____

9.

n	$n \div 6$
3,000	_____
300	_____
_____	5
3	_____

Write the check for each division problem.

10. $40 \div 5 = 8$

    $4 \div 5 = 0.8$

    _____

    _____

11. $3,200 \div 80 = 40$

    $32 \div 80 = 0.4$

    _____

    _____

12. $2,800 \div 40 = 70$

    $28 \div 40 = 0.7$

    _____

    _____

Mixed Review

13. Theresa has 120 bows to make. She can make 6 bows in 10 minutes. How long will it take her to make all of the bows?

14. Sid earns $60 dollars a week. He works 5 hours each week. How much does he earn per hour?

15. 30
    $\times\ 60$

16. 27.45
    $\times\ 0.14$

17. Evaluate $14 + (n + 40)$ for $n = 50$.

Name _____

Decimal Division

Make a model and find the quotient.

1. $0.016 \div 4 =$ _____

2. $\$0.72 \div 8 =$ _____

3. $0.42 \div 6 =$ _____

4. $4.8 \div 8 =$ _____

5. $2.24 \div 4 =$ _____

6. $4.98 \div 6 =$ _____

7. $47.6 \div 7 =$ _____

8. $\$0.18 \div 3 =$ _____

9. $\$1.32 \div 4 =$ _____

10. $22.4 \div 7 =$ _____

11. $0.63 \div 3 =$ _____

12. $3.5 \div 7 =$ _____

Use the model to complete the number sentence.

13. $0.25 \div 5 =$ _____

14. $0.48 \div 4 =$ _____

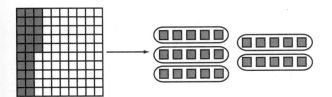
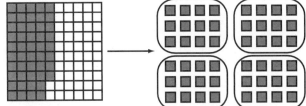

15. $2.8 \div 4 =$ _____

16. $2.4 \div 6 =$ _____

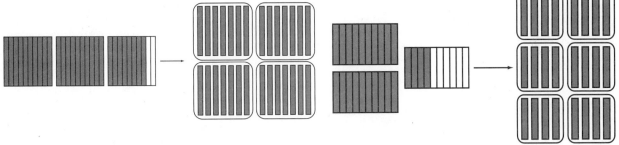

Mixed Review

17.
$$\begin{array}{r} 4.35 \\ \times\ 7.82 \\ \hline \end{array}$$

18.
$$\begin{array}{r} 600 \\ \times\ 90 \\ \hline \end{array}$$

19.
$$\begin{array}{r} 58 \\ \times\ 29 \\ \hline \end{array}$$

20.
$$\begin{array}{r} 368 \\ \times\ 49 \\ \hline \end{array}$$

21.
$$\begin{array}{r} 6.84 \\ \times 0.32 \\ \hline \end{array}$$

22.
$$\begin{array}{r} 487 \\ \times\ 61 \\ \hline \end{array}$$

23. $50\overline{)6{,}875}$

24.
$$\begin{array}{r} 86.84 \\ \times\ 3.24 \\ \hline \end{array}$$

Divide Decimals by Whole Numbers

Copy the quotient and place the decimal point.

1. $\overset{07}{8\overline{)5.6}}$ $8\overline{)5.6}$
2. $\overset{107}{3\overline{)3.21}}$ $3\overline{)3.21}$
3. $\overset{096}{3\overline{)2.88}}$ $3\overline{)2.88}$
4. $\overset{54}{12\overline{)64.8}}$ $12\overline{)64.8}$

5. $\overset{215}{9\overline{)19.35}}$ $9\overline{)19.35}$
6. $\overset{356}{7\overline{)249.2}}$ $7\overline{)249.2}$
7. $\overset{2004}{4\overline{)80.16}}$ $4\overline{)80.16}$
8. $\overset{1467}{5\overline{)73.35}}$ $5\overline{)73.35}$

Find the quotient. Check by multiplying.

9. $7\overline{)47.6}$

10. $2\overline{)6.06}$

11. $3\overline{)2.22}$

12. $14\overline{)\$674.24}$

13. $12\overline{)61.08}$

14. $13\overline{)325.52}$

15. $22.4 \div 7$

16. $237.5 \div 19$

17. $0.63 \div 3$

Mixed Review

18. $4,800 \div 3$

19. $\begin{array}{r} 748.57 \\ + \ 16.38 \\ \hline \end{array}$

20. $\begin{array}{r} 13.406 \\ - \ 1.839 \\ \hline \end{array}$

21. $\begin{array}{r} 76.49 \\ \times \quad 5 \\ \hline \end{array}$

Problem Solving Strategy

Compare Strategies

Work backward or draw a diagram to solve.

1. Mary went shopping for school. She bought 3 pens at $1.75 each and 2 pads of paper for $3.75 each. She paid for these items using one bill. She received $7.25 in change. Was it a $10.00, $20.00, or $50.00 bill?

2. Mark bought two tickets for a show and paid for a dinner. After the show, Mark paid for some snacks. The dinner was $25.00, and each ticket was $12.50. Mark spent $55.00 altogether. How much did he spend on the snacks?

_____

3. The Smythes went on a family vacation and drove 237 miles to Grandma's house. Next they drove 140 miles on each of three days to visit three cousins. When they reached the last cousin's house, the odometer read 48,392.6. What did the odometer read when they started out?

4. Tom and Blair live the same distance from their school. Marcia lives 2 blocks from the school, but 7 blocks from Blair. She lives 1 block closer to the school than she does to Tom. They all live on the same street as the school. How far apart do Tom and Blair live?

_____

Mixed Review

5. Harry needs $160 to buy a bike. He has $70. If he saves $10 each week, how many weeks will it take him to save enough to buy the bike?

6. The difference between two numbers is 3.2. The sum of the numbers is 46.4. What are the two numbers?

_____

7. $\begin{array}{r} 2.29 \\ \times 0.73 \\ \hline \end{array}$

8. $7\overline{)896}$

9. $\begin{array}{r} 16.43 \\ \times 0.809 \\ \hline \end{array}$

10. $13\overline{)411}$

11. $\begin{array}{r} 2,917 \\ \times 18 \\ \hline \end{array}$

Divide to Change a Fraction to a Decimal

Write as a decimal.

1. $\frac{2}{5}$ _____   2. $\frac{7}{10}$ _____   3. $\frac{5}{10}$ _____   4. $\frac{3}{6}$ _____

5. $\frac{2}{8}$ _____   6. $\frac{3}{4}$ _____   7. $\frac{6}{8}$ _____   8. $\frac{3}{20}$ _____

9. $\frac{5}{8}$ _____   10. $\frac{4}{16}$ _____   11. $\frac{12}{20}$ _____   12. $\frac{23}{25}$ _____

13. $\frac{3}{8}$ _____   14. $\frac{21}{40}$ _____   15. $\frac{7}{16}$ _____   16. $\frac{12}{40}$ _____

17. $\frac{51}{80}$ _____   18. $\frac{19}{80}$ _____   19. $\frac{19}{40}$ _____   20. $\frac{7}{20}$ _____

Mixed Review

21. Joanne has $0.66. She has 5 coins. What could they be?

_____

_____

22. Michele was making tuna salad for a party. The recipe for 10 servings called for 8 oz of mayonnaise. A total of 240 people were expected to be at the brunch. How much mayonnaise would Michele need?

_____

23. Order 7.491, 7.049, 7.794 from least to greatest.

_____

24. Round 45.89745 to the nearest ten-thousandths place.

_____

25. How much greater is 24 × 36 than 23 × 35?

_____

26. $\frac{3}{10} + \frac{8}{10} =$ ___   27. $\frac{4}{15} + \frac{7}{15} =$ ___   28. $\frac{10}{12} - \frac{6}{12} =$ ___   29. $\frac{14}{29} - \frac{11}{29} =$ ___

30. $\frac{15}{40} -$ ___ $= \frac{1}{5}$ 31. ___ $+ \frac{13}{52} = \frac{27}{52}$ 32. $\frac{4}{19} +$ ___ $= \frac{11}{19}$ 33. $\frac{17}{20} -$ ___ $= \frac{1}{2}$

Algebra: Patterns in Decimal Division

Complete each multiplication pattern. Then write the related division pattern.

1. $9 \times 7 = 63$

$0.9 \times 7 = $ _____

$0.09 \times 7 = $ _____

_____

_____

_____

2. $68 \times 6 = 408$

$6.8 \times 6 = $ _____

$0.68 \times 6 = $ _____

_____

_____

_____

3. $44 \times 9 = 396$

$4.4 \times 9 = $ _____

$0.44 \times 9 = $ _____

_____

_____

_____

4. $4 \times 5 = 20$

$0.4 \times 5 = $ _____

$0.04 \times 5 = $ _____

_____

_____

_____

5. $73 \times 3 = 219$

$7.3 \times 3 = $ _____

$0.73 \times 3 = $ _____

_____

_____

_____

6. $83 \times 8 = 664$

$8.3 \times 8 = $ _____

$0.83 \times 8 = $ _____

_____

_____

_____

Complete each division pattern.

7. $90 \div 30 = 3$

$9.0 \div 3.0 = $ _____

$0.90 \div 0.30 = $ _____

8. $80 \div 16 = 5$

$8.0 \div 1.6 = $ _____

$0.80 \div 0.16 = $ _____

9. $169 \div 13 = 13$

$16.9 \div 1.3 = $ _____

$1.69 \div 0.13 = $ _____

Algebra Use basic facts and patterns to solve for n.

10. $28 \div 0.04 = n$

_____

11. $0.24 \div 0.08 = n$

_____

12. $3.6 \div n = 0.09$

_____

Mixed Review

13. Write a number that is between 24.56 and 24.60.

_____

14. Estimate the sum of 2,568,986 and 6,234,972 to the nearest hundred thousand.

_____

Divide with Decimals

Make a model to find the quotient. Record a division equation
for each model.

1. $3.6 \div 0.9 =$ _____   **2.** $3.2 \div 0.8 =$ _____   **3.** $2.8 \div 0.7 =$ _____

4. $0.9 \div 0.3 =$ _____   **5.** $0.16 \div 0.02 =$ _____   **6.** $2 \div 0.5 =$ _____

7. $0.42 \div 0.07 =$ _____   **8.** $0.54 \div 0.06 =$ _____   **9.** $0.63 \div 0.07 =$ _____

Use the model. Complete the equation.

10.

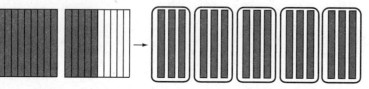

$1.5 \div 0.3 =$ _____

11.

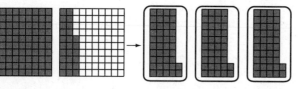

$1.26 \div 0.42 =$ _____

12.

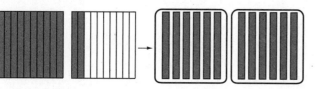

$1.2 \div 0.6 =$ _____

13.

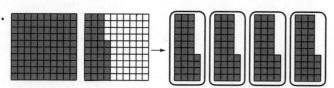

$1.36 \div 0.34 =$ _____

Mixed Review

14. $325.6 \div 4 =$ _____

15.
$$
\begin{array}{r}
423.15 \\
\times \quad 2.3 \\
\hline
\end{array}
$$

16.
$$
\begin{array}{r}
4,347,568 \\
- 2,928,471 \\
\hline
\end{array}
$$

Decimal Division

Place the decimal point in the quotient. Draw arrows to help you.

1. $\overset{12\ 3}{0.5\overline{)6.15}}$

2. $\overset{7\ 2}{0.7\overline{)5.04}}$

3. $\overset{580\ 0}{0.025\overline{)14.50}}$

4. $\overset{42\ 0}{0.08\overline{)3.36}}$

5. $\overset{4\ 9}{0.6\overline{)2.94}}$

6. $\overset{24\ 1}{0.2\overline{)4.82}}$

7. $\overset{4\ 5}{0.5\overline{)2.25}}$

8. $\overset{5\ 9}{0.9\overline{)5.31}}$

Divide.

9. $0.8\overline{)4.16}$

10. $0.6\overline{)2.52}$

11. $0.15\overline{)9.45}$

12. $\$0.45\overline{)\$10.35}$

13. $0.7\overline{)37.1}$

14. $\$0.05\overline{)\$4.65}$

15. $0.9\overline{)2.34}$

16. $0.2\overline{)5.8}$

17. $38.4 \div 2.4$ _____

18. $3.9 \div 1.5$ _____

19. $2.03 \div 0.7$ _____

20. $6.48 \div 1.8$ _____

21. $0.16 \div 0.16$ _____

22. $15.2 \div 0.04$ _____

23. $\$5.12 \div 0.16$ _____

24. $1.04 \div 0.8$ _____

Patterns Divide. Then describe a pattern in the quotients.

25. a. $7.2 \div 1.8$ _____   b. $7.2 \div 0.18$ _____   c. $7.2 \div 0.018$ _____

26. a. $9.6 \div 1.2$ _____   b. $9.6 \div 0.12$ _____   c. $9.6 \div 0.012$ _____

Mixed Review

Solve.

27. $12 + n = 12$

28. $n + 3 = 14$

29. $12 \times n = 144$

30 $n - 7 = 6$

Name _____

Problem Solving Skill

Choose the Operation

Solve. Name the operation or operations you used.

1. An oak tree measured 52 ft high. How many inches would it measure?

2. In 1997 it was estimated that there were 441,297 people living in Charlotte, North Carolina and 195,426 people living in Greensboro, North Carolina. About how many more people lived in Charlotte than in Greensboro?

3. Oranges cost $3.00 a dozen. How much would 3 oranges cost?

4. An elephant takes approximately two years to bear a baby elephant. How many days is that?

There are approximately 28,073 major merchant ships in the world. The United States owns 473 of them, China owns 1,503, Germany owns 472, and Panama owns 4,406, just to name a few.

5. How many more ships does Panama own than Germany and the United States together?

A 2,925
B 3,829
C 3,461
D 1,762

6. What operation would you use to find the total number of ships owned by China, Germany and the United States?

F Multiplication
G Addition
H Subtraction
J Division

Mixed Review

7. Suzanne earned $24.00 for babysitting for 4 hours. How much did she earn in 1 hour?

8. Cindy's dog had a litter of 5 puppies last year and litter of 6 puppies this year. Write an expression for this.

Divisibility

Vocabulary

Fill in the blank.

1. A number is _____ by another number
if the quotient is a whole number and the remainder is zero.

Tell if each number is divisible by 2, 3, 4, 5, 6, 9, or 10.

2. 54   **3.** 144   **4.** 420   **5.** 864

_____   _____   _____   _____

6. 990   **7.** 1,224   **8.** 3,600   **9.** 6,618

_____   _____   _____   _____

10. 234   **11.** 684   **12.** 1,827   **13.** 2,475

_____   _____   _____   _____

14. 675   **15.** 288   **16.** 842   **17.** 540

_____   _____   _____   _____

Mixed Review

18. $9\overline{)37}$ **19.** $44\overline{)794}$ **20.** $0.06 \div 3$ **21.** $0.04 \div 0.2$

_____   _____

22. Marie made 3 dozen cookies.
She needs to divide them evenly
into groups greater than 4. What
are all the possible equal-size
groups into which she can divide
the cookies?

_____

23. Ted needs to divide 60 stickers
into equal groups. What are all
the possible equal-size groups
into which he can divide the
stickers?

_____

Name _____

Name _____

Greatest Common Factor

Vocabulary

Fill in the blanks.

1. The greatest factor that two or more numbers have in common

   is the _____ or _____.

List the factors for each number.

2. 6

3. 20

4. 32

_____   _____   _____

Write the common factors for each set of numbers.

5. 12, 36

6. 4, 20, 24

7. 9, 18, 27

_____   _____   _____

Write the greatest common factor for each set of numbers.

8. 6, 8

   GCF _____

9. 9, 12

   GCF _____

10. 15, 21

    GCF _____

11. 22, 44

    GCF _____

12. 12, 54

    GCF _____

13. 7, 42, 70

    GCF _____

14. 10, 50, 70

    GCF _____

15. 18, 45, 54

    GCF _____

16. 3, 30, 33

    GCF _____

Mixed Review

17. 232
     174
   + 216

18. 872
     704
   + 205

19. 512
     414
   + 781

20. 480
     754
   + 841

21. Evaluate $8 + (3 \times n)$ if $n = 4$.

22. Find the LCM of 3, 4, and 15.

_____   _____

Problem Solving Skill

Identify Relationships

Use the relationships between the given numbers to find the missing number.

1. The GCF of 8 and another number is 1. The LCM is 24. What is the number?

2. The GCF of 9 and another number is 1. The LCM is 45. What is the number?

3. The LCM of 16 and 4 is 16. What is the GCF?

4. The GCF of 13 and 2 is 1. What is the LCM of 13 and 2?

5. The GCF of 9 and 7 is 1. What is the LCM of 9 and 7?

6. The LCM of 9 and 18 is 18. What is the GCF?

7. The GCF of 16 and 12 is 4. What is the LCM of 12 and 16?

8. The LCM of two numbers is 56. What are the numbers?

Mixed Review

9. Evaluate $(n + 3) - 9$ if $n = 15$.

10. $3.2\overline{)9.12}$

11. Write seven million, six hundred thousand, eighty-three in standard form.

12. If a number is divisible by 9, what other number is it also divisible by?

13. $\begin{array}{r} 1,674 \\ \times\ 85 \\ \hline \end{array}$

14. $\begin{array}{r} 6,819 \\ \times\ 5 \\ \hline \end{array}$

15. $\begin{array}{r} 4,242 \\ \times\ 21 \\ \hline \end{array}$

16. $\begin{array}{r} 849 \\ \times\ 69 \\ \hline \end{array}$

Prime and Composite Numbers

Vocabulary

1. A _____ has exactly two factors, 1 and the number itself.

2. A _____ has more than two factors.

Write all the arrays for each number. Write *prime* or *composite* for each number.

3. 8

_____
_____
_____

4. 7

_____
_____
_____

5. 12

_____
_____
_____

6. 9

_____
_____

7. 6

_____
_____

8. 5

_____
_____

Write *prime* or *composite* for each number.

9. 30 _____

10. 16 _____

11. 24 _____

12. 31 _____

Mixed Review

Find the least common multiple for each set of numbers.

13. 6, 7, 3 _____

14. 7, 8, 10 _____

15. 2, 5, 6 _____

16. 3, 4, 7 _____

17. The area of Sharon's garden is 40 sq ft. List all its whole-number possible lengths and widths.

_____
_____

18. Beth has $0.60 more than Suzy. Together they have $8.20. How much money does each girl have?

_____
_____

Name _____

Introduction to Exponents

Write in exponent form.

1. 10,000,000,000

2. 100,000

3. 100,000,000

_____

_____

_____

4. 1,000,000,000

5. 10,000

6. 100,000,000,000

_____

_____

_____

Find the value.

7. 10^9

8. 10^6

9. 10^4

_____

_____

_____

10. 10^5

11. 10^7

12. 10^{10}

_____

_____

_____

Find the value of *n*.

13. $10 \times n \times 10 = 10^3$

14. $100{,}000 = 10^n$

15. $1{,}000{,}000 = 10^n$

_____

_____

_____

Compare. Write $<$, $>$, or $=$ in each ☐.

16. 10,000 ☐ 10^5

17. 10^4 ☐ 10,000

18. 10×100 ☐ 10^3

Mixed Review

Order from *least* to *greatest*.

19. 1.939, 1.393, 3.919, 91.93, 3.199

Order from *greatest* to *least*.

20. 2.345, 2.543, 2.435, 2.534, 2.453

_____

_____

Compare. Write $<$, $>$, or $=$ in each ☐.

21. 5.9376 ☐ 5.3897

22. 8.639 ☐ 8,639

23. 3,384,844 ☐ 3,038,484

24. William gives $\frac{3}{6}$ of his energy bar to James and $\frac{1}{2}$ to Phyllis. How much does William have left?

25. What type of graph would you use to display the ages of students in your classroom?

_____

_____

PW80 Practice

Evaluate Expressions with Exponents

Write the equal factors.

1. 9^3

2. 7^6

3. 12^5

4. 21^4

_____   _____   _____   _____

_____   _____   _____   _____

Write each expression by using an exponent.

5. $6 \times 6 \times 6 \times 6 \times 6 \times 6 \times 6 \times 6$

6. $75 \times 75 \times 75 \times 75 \times 75$

_____   _____

7. $53 \times 53 \times 53 \times 53 \times 53 \times 53 \times 53$

8. $9 \times 9 \times 9 \times 9 \times 9 \times 9$

_____   _____

Find the value.

9. 14^2

10. 6^4

11. 3^6

12. 12^3

_____   _____   _____   _____

13. 7^4

14. 1^{10}

15. 11^5

16. 42^2

_____   _____   _____   _____

Find the value of n.

17. $n^4 = 16$

18. $6^n = 216$

19. $5^n = 625$

20. $11^n = 1,331$

_____   _____   _____   _____

Mixed Review

Solve.

21. $3,302$
    $\times \quad 41$

22. $45\overline{)2,025}$

23. $1,296$
    $\times \quad 36$

24. $36\overline{)46,656}$

25. $7,905$
    $\times \quad 62$

26. $17\overline{)9,520}$

27. $5,461$
    $\times \quad 33$

28. $29\overline{)24,418}$

Name _____

Exponents and Prime Factors

Complete.

1. $36 = 2 \times \square \times 3 \times \square$

_____

2. $9 \times 4 = \square \times \square \times \square \times 2$

_____

3. $44 = \square \times 2 \times 11$

_____

4. $48 = 2 \times \square \times \square \times \square \times 3$

_____

Rewrite by using exponents.

5. $3 \times 5 \times 3 \times 5$

_____

6. $6 \times 6 \times 6 \times 4 \times 4$

_____

7. $2 \times 2 \times 3 \times 2 \times 3 \times 2$

_____

8. $8 \times 4 \times 4 \times 8 \times 4$

_____

9. $5 \times 5 \times 5 \times 5 \times 13$

_____

10. $64 \times 64 \times 64 \times 64$

_____

Find the prime factorization of the number. Use exponents when possible.

11. 32

_____

12. 49

_____

13. 54

_____

14. 81

_____

15. 144

_____

16. 256

_____

Complete the prime factorization. Find the value of the variable.

17. $5 \times 5 \times 5 \times 5 = 5^n$

_____

18. $3^2 \times n = 36$

_____

19. $5^2 \times 5^r = 625$

_____

20. $7 \times 7 \times 2^w = 392$

_____

21. $2 \times 3 \times 5^d = 150$

_____

22. $13^m \times 2^4 = 208$

_____

Mixed Review

23. $\begin{array}{r} 8,142 \\ +\ 7,539 \\ \hline \end{array}$

24. $4\overline{)256}$

25. $\begin{array}{r} 42,877 \\ -\ 21,759 \\ \hline \end{array}$

26. $\begin{array}{r} 3,458 \\ \times\quad 36 \\ \hline \end{array}$

Relate Decimals to Fractions

Write a fraction for each decimal.

1. 0.2

2. 0.14

3. 0.127

4. 0.68

_____

_____

_____

_____

5. 0.05

6. 0.84

7. 0.8

8. 0.28

_____

_____

_____

_____

9. 0.01

10. 0.678

11. 0.35

12. 0.61

_____

_____

_____

_____

Write a decimal for each fraction.

13. $\frac{6}{10}$

14. $\frac{83}{100}$

15. $\frac{39}{100}$

16. $\frac{645}{1,000}$

_____

_____

_____

_____

17. $\frac{3}{10}$

18. $\frac{1}{100}$

19. $\frac{71}{100}$

20. $\frac{16}{1,000}$

_____

_____

_____

_____

21. $\frac{5}{10}$

22. $\frac{12}{100}$

23. $\frac{199}{1,000}$

24. $\frac{33}{100}$

_____

_____

_____

_____

Mixed Review

25. $\begin{array}{r} 122 \\ 174 \\ +\ 296 \\ \hline \end{array}$

26. $\begin{array}{r} 138 \\ 104 \\ +\ 186 \\ \hline \end{array}$

27. $\begin{array}{r} 1,302 \\ +\ 2,996 \\ \hline \end{array}$

28. $\begin{array}{r} 21.2 \\ 7.9 \\ +\ 39.6 \\ \hline \end{array}$

29. $\begin{array}{r} 13,274 \\ -\ 2,016 \\ \hline \end{array}$

30. $\begin{array}{r} 7,520 \\ +\ 1,381 \\ \hline \end{array}$

31. $\begin{array}{r} 67,794 \\ -\ 5,418 \\ \hline \end{array}$

32. $\begin{array}{r} 23,681 \\ +\ 99,875 \\ \hline \end{array}$

33. $\begin{array}{r} 779 \\ \times\ \ 6 \\ \hline \end{array}$

34. $\begin{array}{r} 4,782 \\ \times\ \ \ \ 3 \\ \hline \end{array}$

35. $\begin{array}{r} 48,119 \\ \times\ \ \ \ \ \ 7 \\ \hline \end{array}$

36. $\begin{array}{r} 361,195 \\ \times\ \ \ \ \ \ \ 5 \\ \hline \end{array}$

Name _____

Equivalent Fractions

Use the number lines to name an equivalent fraction for each.

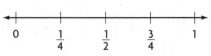

1. $\frac{1}{4}$ _____

2. $\frac{4}{8}$ _____

3. $\frac{3}{4}$ _____

Write an equivalent fraction. Use multiplication or division.

4. $\frac{2}{4}$ _____

5. $\frac{18}{20}$ _____

6. $\frac{3}{8}$ _____

7. $\frac{7}{21}$ _____

8. $\frac{3}{5}$ _____

9. $\frac{2}{15}$ _____

10. $\frac{8}{12}$ _____

11. $\frac{10}{16}$ _____

Which fraction is *not* equivalent to the given fraction? Circle *a, b,* or *c.*

12. $\frac{2}{3}$ a. $\frac{6}{9}$ b. $\frac{5}{6}$ c. $\frac{8}{12}$

13. $\frac{9}{15}$ a. $\frac{3}{5}$ b. $\frac{18}{30}$ c. $\frac{16}{25}$

14. $\frac{6}{8}$ a. $\frac{10}{12}$ b. $\frac{3}{4}$ c. $\frac{24}{32}$

15. $\frac{3}{7}$ a. $\frac{6}{14}$ b. $\frac{14}{28}$ c. $\frac{21}{49}$

Mixed Review

16. René and 6 friends decide to order lasagna. Each tray of lasagna is cut into 12 pieces. How many trays of lasagna will they have to buy in order for everyone to get 3 pieces? How many pieces will be left over?

_____

_____

17. Andy bought a pack of 16 pencils and gave 4 pencils away to friends. Write two equivalent fractions to represent the part of the pencils that Andy gave away.

_____

Solve the equation.

18. $5 \times n = 60$

19. $60 \div n = 6$

20. $75 + n = 90$

21. $n - 3 = 9$

_____   _____   _____   _____

22. $n \times 8 = 32$

23. $144 \div n = 12$

24. $26 + n = 64$

25. $18 - n = 7$

_____   _____   _____   _____

PW84   Practice

Compare and Order Fractions

Rename, using the LCM, and compare.
Write $<$, $>$, or $=$ in each $\bigcirc$.

1. $\frac{3}{12} \bigcirc \frac{5}{8}$
2. $\frac{2}{8} \bigcirc \frac{7}{32}$
3. $\frac{6}{8} \bigcirc \frac{3}{9}$
4. $\frac{2}{3} \bigcirc \frac{6}{9}$

5. $\frac{5}{6} \bigcirc \frac{3}{4}$
6. $\frac{3}{15} \bigcirc \frac{1}{3}$
7. $\frac{6}{22} \bigcirc \frac{3}{11}$
8. $\frac{3}{7} \bigcirc \frac{6}{21}$

9. $\frac{5}{6} \bigcirc \frac{5}{8}$
10. $\frac{3}{7} \bigcirc \frac{11}{14}$
11. $\frac{7}{12} \bigcirc \frac{3}{8}$
12. $\frac{9}{10} \bigcirc \frac{6}{7}$

13. $\frac{12}{40} \bigcirc \frac{6}{10}$
14. $\frac{4}{5} \bigcirc \frac{2}{4}$
15. $\frac{4}{7} \bigcirc \frac{1}{2}$
16. $\frac{3}{4} \bigcirc \frac{8}{9}$

Write in order from least to greatest.

17. $\frac{2}{5}, \frac{2}{3}, \frac{4}{15}$

18. $\frac{2}{3}, \frac{3}{4}, \frac{7}{12}$

19. $\frac{7}{9}, \frac{1}{2}, \frac{11}{18}$

_____

20. $\frac{5}{6}, \frac{1}{4}, \frac{5}{12}$

21. $\frac{4}{5}, \frac{7}{10}, \frac{1}{2}$

22. $\frac{9}{15}, \frac{2}{3}, \frac{2}{5}$

_____

Mixed Review

23. 16×15

24. $2\overline{)698}$

25. $5.7 + 6.8$

26. 1.2×3

_____

27. $20 + (30 - 2)$

28. 28×26

29. $67 - 28$

30. $6.6 + 7.8$

_____

31. Petra loves animals. She has twelve pets in all, four of which are rabbits. Write a fraction to describe the number of rabbits she has.

32. Flora's Flowers sells 3 roses for $13.50. The Green Thumb sells 4 roses for $15.00. Discount Flowers sells 6 roses for $23.00. Who sells roses at the lowest price?

Simplest Form

Tell whether the fraction is in simplest form. Write *yes* or *no*.

1. $\frac{3}{4}$ _____

2. $\frac{6}{8}$ _____

3. $\frac{7}{21}$ _____

4. $\frac{14}{15}$ _____

5. $\frac{12}{15}$ _____

6. $\frac{7}{9}$ _____

Write each fraction in simplest form.

7. $\frac{4}{10}$ _____

8. $\frac{3}{8}$ _____

9. $\frac{6}{12}$ _____

10. $\frac{6}{15}$ _____

11. $\frac{2}{3}$ _____

12. $\frac{4}{16}$ _____

13. $\frac{2}{8}$ _____

14. $\frac{8}{12}$ _____

15. $\frac{8}{24}$ _____

16. $\frac{3}{9}$ _____

17. $\frac{4}{15}$ _____

18. $\frac{7}{17}$ _____

Mixed Review

Solve.

19. $3,000 \div 100$

20. $485 \div 100$

21. $48,000 \div 200$

22. 15.68×3

_____   _____   _____   _____

23. Jean-Paul uses $\frac{1}{3}$ cup walnuts, $\frac{1}{8}$ cup chocolate chips, and $\frac{1}{2}$ cup coconut in his cookie recipe. Which of these ingredients does he use the most? Use fraction bars to explain your answer.

_____

_____

_____

24. Mary ran $\frac{3}{4}$ mile, Lila ran $\frac{2}{3}$ mile, and Sue ran $\frac{3}{8}$ mile. Who ran the farthest? Draw a diagram to solve.

_____

Understand Mixed Numbers

Vocabulary

Complete.

1. A _____ is made up of a
   whole number and a fraction.

For 2–5, use the figures at the right.

2. How many whole figures are
   shaded?

   _____

3. Into how many parts is each
   figure divided?

   _____

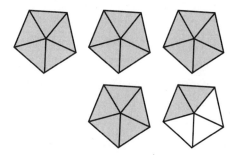

4. How many parts of the last
   figure are shaded?

   _____

5. Write a fraction and a mixed
   number for the figures.

   _____

Write each fraction as a mixed number.

6. $\frac{22}{7}$ _____

7. $\frac{7}{5}$ _____

8. $\frac{19}{4}$ _____

9. $\frac{13}{2}$ _____

Write each mixed number as a fraction.

10. $4\frac{2}{3}$ _____

11. $1\frac{4}{6}$ _____

12. $3\frac{2}{5}$ _____

13. $2\frac{2}{4}$ _____

Mixed Review

14. Sam watched 10 cars drive past
    him. Of those cars, 6 were white.
    Write a fraction to describe the
    fraction of white cars.

15. Maria takes 6 classes. In 5 of
    those classes, she has an A.
    Write a fraction to describe the
    fraction of classes in which she
    has an A.

_____

_____

Problem Solving Strategy

Make a Model

Make a model to solve.

1. Samantha bought 3 packets of stickers. Each packet contains 100 stickers. If she divides all of the stickers evenly among 6 friends and herself, how many stickers are left over?

_____

2. One day, $\frac{2}{8}$ of the patients brought to a veterinary hospital were rabbits, $\frac{1}{2}$ were cats, and $\frac{1}{4}$ were dogs. Which kind of animal did the vet see the most of that day?

_____

3. James uses $\frac{5}{6}$ meter of butcher paper to make one sign. How many meters of paper will he need to make 3 signs?

_____

4. Brent decorated $\frac{1}{6}$ of his sugar cookies with blue frosting, $\frac{1}{4}$ with yellow frosting, and $\frac{3}{8}$ with purple frosting. Which frosting was used the least?

_____

Mixed Review

Solve.

5. During the week, Carrie spent $3.50 for a book. The next day her father gave her $1.25. Then she went to a movie, which cost $7.50. If she now has $10.25, how much money did she have at the beginning of the week?

_____

6. A pizza parlor has a special offer of a mini-pizza with one topping. Customers can choose thin or thick crust, and they have 4 choices of toppings: pepperoni, sausage, extra cheese, or olives. How many choices do customers have?

_____

7. $64 \div n = 8$

_____

8. $63 \div 3 = n$

_____

9. $121 \div n = 11$

_____

10. $n \div 7 = 7$

_____

Name _____

Add and Subtract Like Fractions

Find the sum or difference. Write it in simplest form.

1. $\frac{5}{7} + \frac{1}{7}$

2. $\frac{4}{9} + \frac{3}{9}$

3. $\frac{4}{12} + \frac{8}{12}$

4. $\frac{3}{11} + \frac{7}{11}$

_____ _____ _____ _____

5. $\frac{2}{8} + \frac{4}{8}$

6. $\frac{7}{15} + \frac{4}{15}$

7. $\frac{5}{9} + \frac{1}{9}$

8. $\frac{1}{4} + \frac{2}{4}$

_____ _____ _____ _____

9. $\frac{4}{7} - \frac{2}{7}$

10. $\frac{3}{5} - \frac{1}{5}$

11. $\frac{6}{12} - \frac{2}{12}$

12. $\frac{3}{4} - \frac{2}{4}$

_____ _____ _____ _____

13. $\frac{7}{9} - \frac{2}{9}$

14. $\frac{4}{6} - \frac{1}{6}$

15. $\frac{3}{8} - \frac{2}{8}$

16. $\frac{9}{10} - \frac{5}{10}$

_____ _____ _____ _____

17. George ran $\frac{3}{8}$ mile on Sunday and $\frac{2}{8}$ mile on Monday. How much farther did George run on Sunday than on Monday?

_____

18. Lona pulled the wagon for $\frac{4}{10}$ hour. Eric pulled the wagon for $\frac{1}{10}$ hour. For how long did they pull the wagon in all?

_____

Mixed Review

19. 396 × 54

20. 603,421 − 82,798

21. 1.62 × 66

22. 0.26 × 0.29

23. $27\overline{)28.35}$

24. $18\overline{)1,368}$

Add Unlike Fractions

Use fraction bars to find the sum.

1.
$\frac{1}{3}$	$\frac{1}{3}$	$\frac{1}{6}$

_____

2.
$\frac{1}{4}$	$\frac{1}{4}$	$\frac{1}{8}$	$\frac{1}{8}$	$\frac{1}{8}$

_____

3.
$\frac{1}{3}$	$\frac{1}{3}$	$\frac{1}{4}$

_____

4.
$\frac{1}{2}$	$\frac{1}{5}$

_____

5.
$\frac{1}{12}$	$\frac{1}{12}$	$\frac{1}{12}$	$\frac{1}{3}$

_____

6.
$\frac{1}{10}$	$\frac{1}{10}$	$\frac{1}{10}$	$\frac{1}{5}$

_____

7. $\dfrac{1}{3} + \dfrac{1}{6}$

_____

8. $\dfrac{5}{8} + \dfrac{1}{4}$

_____

9. $\dfrac{3}{4} + \dfrac{1}{6}$

_____

10. $\dfrac{7}{10} + \dfrac{1}{5}$

_____

11. $\dfrac{4}{10} + \dfrac{1}{5}$

_____

12. $\dfrac{1}{5} + \dfrac{7}{10}$

_____

Mixed Review

13. $\dfrac{1}{9} + \dfrac{4}{9}$

_____

14. $\dfrac{7}{16} - \dfrac{3}{16}$

_____

15. $\dfrac{3}{8} + \dfrac{3}{8}$

_____

16. $\dfrac{9}{12} - \dfrac{4}{12}$

_____

17. $\begin{array}{r} 4{,}913 \\ \times\ \ \ 16 \\ \hline \end{array}$

18. $\begin{array}{r} 56{,}794 \\ -\ 21{,}879 \\ \hline \end{array}$

19. $\begin{array}{r} 0.84 \\ \times\ \ 15 \\ \hline \end{array}$

20. $7\overline{)869.68}$

21. $\begin{array}{r} 77.4 \\ \times\ 1.8 \\ \hline \end{array}$

22. $\begin{array}{r} 150{,}631 \\ +\ 49{,}495 \\ \hline \end{array}$

23. $\begin{array}{r} 39.6 \\ \times\ 0.8 \\ \hline \end{array}$

24. $\begin{array}{r} 19.99 \\ +\ 6.51 \\ \hline \end{array}$

Subtract Unlike Fractions

Use fraction bars to find the difference.

1.

2.

3.

_____

_____

_____

4.

5.

6.

_____

_____

_____

7. $\dfrac{4}{5} - \dfrac{3}{10}$

8. $\dfrac{4}{6} - \dfrac{5}{12}$

9. $\dfrac{5}{6} - \dfrac{5}{12}$

_____

_____

_____

10. $\dfrac{1}{2} - \dfrac{4}{10}$

11. $\dfrac{6}{8} - \dfrac{1}{2}$

12. $\dfrac{2}{3} - \dfrac{3}{6}$

_____

_____

_____

13. $\dfrac{1}{2} - \dfrac{1}{8}$

14. $\dfrac{9}{12} - \dfrac{2}{3}$

15. $\dfrac{4}{6} - \dfrac{1}{12}$

_____

_____

_____

16. $\dfrac{7}{8} - \dfrac{1}{4}$

17. $\dfrac{11}{12} - \dfrac{1}{3}$

18. $\dfrac{4}{6} - \dfrac{1}{2}$

_____

_____

_____

Mixed Review

19.
$$\begin{array}{r} \$936.42 \\ \times \quad\quad 13 \\ \hline \end{array}$$

20. $5\overline{)11{,}045}$

21.
$$\begin{array}{r} 1.372 \\ \times \quad 1.3 \\ \hline \end{array}$$

22. $9\overline{)48.6}$

23. 12×6 _____

24. 12×11 _____

25. 12×10 _____

26. 12×9 _____

Estimate Sums and Differences

Write whether the fraction is closest to 0, $\frac{1}{2}$, or 1.

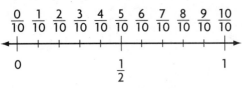

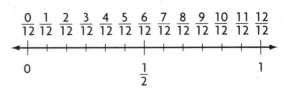

1. $\frac{4}{10}$ 2. $\frac{11}{12}$ 3. $\frac{2}{10}$ 4. $\frac{7}{12}$

_____   _____   _____   _____

5. $\frac{7}{8}$ 6. $\frac{3}{8}$ 7. $\frac{2}{9}$ 8. $\frac{1}{8}$

_____   _____   _____   _____

Estimate each sum or difference.

9. $\frac{1}{2} + \frac{3}{4}$ 10. $\frac{1}{2} + \frac{5}{8}$ 11. $\frac{1}{4} + \frac{5}{9}$ 12. $\frac{6}{8} + \frac{2}{4}$

_____   _____   _____   _____

13. $\frac{11}{12} - \frac{1}{9}$ 14. $\frac{5}{6} - \frac{3}{5}$ 15. $\frac{8}{9} - \frac{3}{4}$ 16. $\frac{7}{9} - \frac{5}{8}$

_____   _____   _____   _____

Estimate to compare. Write $<$ or $>$ in each $\bigcirc$.

17. $\frac{5}{8} + \frac{2}{8} \bigcirc \frac{1}{5} + \frac{2}{5}$ 18. $\frac{6}{7} - \frac{3}{8} \bigcirc \frac{7}{9} - \frac{3}{4}$

19. $\frac{6}{9} + \frac{3}{5} \bigcirc \frac{7}{8} + \frac{3}{5}$ 20. $\frac{5}{6} - \frac{1}{4} \bigcirc \frac{3}{6} - \frac{1}{3}$

Mixed Review

21. $14\overline{)37.38}$ 22. $56{,}789 \times 17$ 23. 76.18×204 24. $0.07\overline{)3.0086}$

Name _____

Use Least Common Denominators

Name the LCD. Then add or subtract.

1. $1 - \dfrac{3}{4}$

2. $\dfrac{2}{3} + \dfrac{3}{4}$

3. $\dfrac{9}{10} - \dfrac{2}{5}$

4. $\dfrac{3}{4} - \dfrac{2}{5}$

_____   _____   _____   _____

Find the sum or difference.

5. $\dfrac{1}{9} + \dfrac{2}{3}$

6. $\dfrac{6}{8} - \dfrac{1}{2}$

7. $\dfrac{3}{4} - \dfrac{5}{16}$

8. $\dfrac{3}{5} - \dfrac{3}{10}$

_____   _____   _____   _____

9. $\dfrac{5}{12} + \dfrac{1}{3}$

10. $\dfrac{7}{8} - \dfrac{1}{4}$

11. $\dfrac{2}{3} + \dfrac{1}{5}$

12. $\dfrac{5}{7} - \dfrac{1}{3}$

_____   _____   _____   _____

Find the value of n.

13. $\dfrac{3}{4} + n = 1$

14. $\dfrac{7}{8} - n = \dfrac{3}{8}$

15. $\dfrac{3}{10} + n = \dfrac{7}{10}$

16. $n - \dfrac{3}{5} = \dfrac{1}{2}$

_____   _____   _____   _____

17. $n + \dfrac{5}{12} = \dfrac{7}{12}$

18. $\dfrac{3}{16} + n = \dfrac{7}{16}$

19. $\dfrac{1}{2} - n = \dfrac{3}{8}$

20. $\dfrac{3}{4} - n = \dfrac{9}{12}$

_____   _____   _____   _____

Mixed Review

Name the least common multiple (LCM).

21. 6 and 8 _____

22. 2 and 7 _____

23. 3 and 9 _____

Solve.

24. $1,328 \div 83$ _____

25. $\begin{array}{r} 257,769 \\ + 44,883 \\ \hline \end{array}$

26. $\begin{array}{r} 42,789 \\ \times \quad 56 \\ \hline \end{array}$

Add and Subtract Unlike Fractions

Find the LCD. Then add or subtract.

1. $\dfrac{1}{2} + \dfrac{2}{8}$

2. $\dfrac{2}{5} + \dfrac{1}{3}$

3. $\dfrac{6}{8} + \dfrac{1}{4}$

4. $\dfrac{9}{12} - \dfrac{2}{4}$

_____   _____   _____   _____

Find the sum or difference. Write the answer in simplest form.

5. $\dfrac{8}{16} - \dfrac{2}{8}$

6. $\dfrac{2}{10} + \dfrac{3}{5}$

7. $\dfrac{7}{9} - \dfrac{1}{3}$

8. $\dfrac{4}{15} + \dfrac{2}{3}$

_____   _____   _____   _____

9. $\dfrac{3}{8} - \dfrac{1}{4}$

10. $\dfrac{6}{12} - \dfrac{2}{6}$

11. $\dfrac{9}{10} - \dfrac{4}{5}$

12. $\dfrac{6}{8} - \dfrac{1}{2}$

_____   _____   _____   _____

13. $\dfrac{5}{8} + \dfrac{5}{16}$

14. $\dfrac{4}{5} + \dfrac{1}{10}$

15. $\dfrac{5}{9} - \dfrac{7}{18}$

16. $\dfrac{1}{2} - \dfrac{3}{14}$

_____   _____   _____   _____

17. $\dfrac{2}{20} + \dfrac{4}{5}$

18. $\dfrac{1}{3} - \dfrac{2}{9}$

19. $\dfrac{2}{6} - \dfrac{5}{18}$

20. $\dfrac{3}{8} + \dfrac{2}{4}$

_____   _____   _____   _____

Mixed Review

21. Jade swam $\frac{1}{2}$ mile on Monday. On Wednesday she swam $\frac{3}{8}$ mile. How many miles did Jade swim in all?

22. Monty spent $\frac{4}{5}$ hour mowing his lawn. Then he spent $\frac{2}{10}$ hour mowing his neighbor's lawn. How much longer did it take Monty to mow his lawn than his neighbor's lawn?

_____   _____

23. $14\overline{)39.9}$

24. $\begin{array}{r} 367{,}112 \\ \times 60 \\ \hline \end{array}$

25. $\dfrac{1}{4} + \dfrac{3}{4}$

26. $\begin{array}{r} 36.725 \\ -14.294 \\ \hline \end{array}$

Problem Solving Strategy

Work Backward

Work backward to solve.

1. Jerry's kitten is 19 cm tall and is 6 months old. The kitten grew 2 cm between the ages of 5 months and 6 months. It grew 3 cm between the ages of 4 months and 5 months. How tall was Jerry's kitten when it was 4 months old?

_____

2. Denise went shopping at the mall. She spent $11.35 on a new T-shirt and $2.25 for hair ribbons. Lunch cost $4.50, and a drink cost $1.25. She came home with $10.65. How much money did Denise have before she went to the mall?

_____

3. Kirk grew a crystal in science class. On Monday it was $\frac{13}{16}$ inch tall. It had grown $\frac{1}{4}$ inch between Friday and Monday. It had grown $\frac{1}{2}$ inch between Tuesday and Friday. How tall was Kirk's crystal on Tuesday?

_____

4. Terry planted a gladiolus bulb. On Wednesday it was $\frac{7}{8}$ inch tall. It had grown $\frac{1}{4}$ inch between Tuesday and Wednesday. It had grown $\frac{3}{8}$ inch between Monday and Tuesday. How tall was Terry's gladiolus on Monday?

_____

Mixed Review

Write the value of the 4 in each of these numbers.

5. 14,790.12

6. 0.4913

7. 499,765,315

8. 0.045

_____   _____   _____   _____

Solve.

9.	10.	11.	12.
4.80	17.59	19,515	$15.99
6.62	33.81	7,563	15.99
+ 9.90	+ 67.08	+ 27,480	+ 15.99

Add Mixed Numbers

Find the sum in simplest form. Estimate to check.

1. $2\frac{3}{8}$
   $+3\frac{1}{4}$

2. $4\frac{1}{3}$
   $+3\frac{1}{6}$

3. $1\frac{5}{12}$
   $+2\frac{1}{6}$

4. $3\frac{5}{8}$
   $+3\frac{3}{4}$

5. $1\frac{1}{10}$
   $+4\frac{2}{5}$

6. $3\frac{1}{9}$
   $+4\frac{1}{3}$

7. $2\frac{3}{5}$
   $+5\frac{7}{10}$

8. $4\frac{1}{12}$
   $+2\frac{1}{3}$

Algebra Find the value of n.

9. $3\frac{1}{4} + 3\frac{7}{8} = n$ _____

10. $n + 5\frac{3}{10} = 8\frac{1}{10}$ _____

11. $7\frac{2}{3} + n = 9\frac{1}{12}$ _____

12. $2\frac{2}{3} + n = 6\frac{5}{6}$ _____

13. $n + 3\frac{5}{6} = 5\frac{1}{3}$ _____

14. $n + n = 8\frac{1}{2}$ _____

15. $5\frac{5}{12} + 2\frac{1}{6} = n$ _____

16. $8\frac{2}{9} + n = 9\frac{5}{9}$ _____

Mixed Review

17. Tim and Al are making a tower. They each built a separate section. Tim's section was $\frac{7}{8}$ foot tall, and Al's section was $\frac{1}{2}$ foot tall. How tall will the tower be when they join the sections?

_____

18. Harriet and Felicia worked for the local charity. Harriet worked 5 hours, and Felicia worked 3 hours more than Harriet. How many hours did the girls work for the charity altogether?

_____

19. 21.376
    $+ 9.653$

20. 145.637
    $- 18.910$

21. $\$10 + (\$6 - n)$ if $n = \$3$ _____

22. $5(3 \times 7) = n$ _____

Subtract Mixed Numbers

Find the difference in simplest form. Estimate to check.

1. $3\frac{7}{10}$
   $-1\frac{2}{5}$
   _____

2. $5\frac{3}{4}$
   $-2\frac{1}{8}$
   _____

3. $8\frac{5}{6}$
   $-2\frac{1}{12}$
   _____

4. $7\frac{1}{2}$
   $-4\frac{1}{6}$
   _____

5. $9\frac{9}{10}$
   $-4\frac{3}{5}$
   _____

6. $5\frac{4}{9}$
   $-3\frac{1}{3}$
   _____

Algebra Find the value of n.

7. $4\frac{7}{8} - 2\frac{3}{4} = n$ _____

8. $5\frac{4}{5} - 3\frac{n}{5} = 2\frac{1}{5}$ _____

9. $n - 2\frac{1}{4} = 1\frac{1}{6}$ _____

10. $5\frac{7}{12} - 3\frac{6}{n} = 2\frac{1}{12}$ _____

11. $9\frac{5}{6} - n = 5\frac{1}{6}$ _____

12. $7\frac{3}{8} - n = 5\frac{1}{8}$ _____

13. $6\frac{3}{4} - 4\frac{n}{4} = 2\frac{1}{2}$ _____

14. $3\frac{6}{8} - 2\frac{5}{n} = 1\frac{1}{8}$ _____

Mixed Review

15. Sam made the table at the right to keep track of how much wood he had for projects. He forgot to enter some of the numbers. Complete the table.

16. Each week Sam will work $3\frac{1}{2}$ hours on Wednesday and $4\frac{1}{4}$ hours on Friday. How many hours will he work each week?

_____

WOOD FOR PROJECTS			
Type of Wood	Feet Started With	Feet Used	Feet Left
Oak	$15\frac{1}{2}$	$9\frac{1}{4}$	_____
Pine	$22\frac{5}{8}$	_____	$10\frac{1}{4}$
Maple	_____	$12\frac{3}{4}$	$2\frac{1}{6}$
Cherry	$20\frac{3}{4}$	$5\frac{3}{8}$	

Subtraction With Renaming

Use fraction bars to find the difference.

1. $3\frac{2}{3}$
    $-\ \frac{1}{6}$

2. $7\frac{1}{4}$
    $-3\frac{3}{8}$

3. $4\frac{3}{10}$
    $-2\frac{4}{5}$

4. $6\frac{2}{3}$
    $-4\frac{5}{6}$

5. $8\frac{1}{2}$
    $-1\frac{5}{6}$

6. $3\frac{1}{8}$
    $-1\frac{1}{2}$

7. $7\frac{1}{10}$
    $-4\frac{2}{5}$

8. $10\frac{3}{8}$
    $-\ 5\frac{3}{4}$

9. $6\frac{11}{12} - 2\frac{2}{3}$ _____

10. $4\frac{1}{5} - 1\frac{7}{10}$ _____

11. $5\frac{5}{8} - 1\frac{3}{4}$ _____

12. $5\frac{1}{2} - 2\frac{7}{12}$ _____

13. $8\frac{1}{6} - 4\frac{5}{12}$ _____

14. $7\frac{1}{4} - 6\frac{7}{12}$ _____

Mixed Review

15. Stacey had 3 cakes for her party. She had $\frac{1}{8}$ of a cake left after the party. How much cake was eaten at her party?

_____

16. Martha spent $2\frac{1}{2}$ hours reading on Saturday. She spent $\frac{3}{4}$ of an hour reading on Sunday. How many hours did she spend reading this weekend?

_____

17. $0.3\overline{)144.9}$

18. $76{,}592$
    $\times\ \ \ \ \ 104$

19. $n \times 11 = 77$ _____

20. $\frac{6}{9} - \frac{1}{3} =$ _____

21. $256{,}719$
    $\times\ \ \ \ \ 0.3$

22. $\frac{7}{12} - \frac{3}{12} =$ _____

23. $12\overline{)543.6}$

Name _____

Practice with Mixed Numbers

Add or subtract. Write the answer in simplest form. Estimate to check.

1. $3\frac{1}{4}$
    $-2\frac{7}{8}$

2. $2\frac{1}{2}$
    $-1\frac{3}{5}$

3. $5\frac{7}{12}$
    $+3\frac{1}{8}$

4. $5\frac{3}{8}$
    $-1\frac{5}{16}$

5. $8\frac{9}{10}$
    $-5\frac{1}{5}$

6. $9\frac{2}{8}$
    $+3\frac{5}{12}$

7. $6\frac{4}{9}$
    $+10\frac{3}{18}$

8. $6\frac{2}{3}$
    $-2\frac{1}{12}$

9. $7\frac{2}{3}$
    $+1\frac{5}{12}$

10. $8\frac{5}{9}$
    $-3\frac{1}{3}$

11. $5\frac{5}{12}$
    $+2\frac{1}{6}$

12. $12\frac{1}{2}$
    $-4\frac{1}{3}$

Algebra Find the value of n.

13. $3\frac{1}{4} + n = 7\frac{1}{8}$ _____

14. $6\frac{5}{6} - n = 2\frac{2}{3}$ _____

15. $9\frac{5}{9} - n = 8\frac{2}{9}$ _____

16. $n + 4\frac{2}{3} = 8\frac{1}{2}$ _____

Mixed Review

17. Write $\frac{7}{8}$ as a decimal. _____

18. $3.78 + n$ if $n = 4.59$ _____

19. $0.7)\overline{6.58}$

20. $\frac{1}{5} + \frac{4}{5}$ _____

21. Find the greatest common factor of 36 and 60.

_____

22. Find the least common multiple of 8 and 10.

_____

Problem Solving Skill

Multistep Problems

1. Emily used wallpaper border to outline her window. She used $6\frac{1}{3}$ yards to outline the door and $1\frac{1}{6}$ yards to outline a shelf. She used $9\frac{1}{2}$ yards of border in all. How much border did she use for the window?

_____

2. On Friday Jake had done a total of 125 push-ups in five days. He did 20 on Monday, 30 on Tuesday, 15 on Wednesday, and 20 on Thursday. How many push-ups did he do on Friday?

_____

3. Dirk spent $3\frac{3}{4}$ hours outside on Saturday. During that time he spent $1\frac{1}{2}$ hours at the park and $1\frac{1}{4}$ hours in a friend's yard. He also rode his bicycle. How much time did he spend riding his bicycle?

_____

4. Terry saved $60 to spend on a party for her mother. She spent $25 for a cake and $12 for party decorations. She spent the rest on a gift. How much did she spend on the gift?

_____

Mixed Review

Solve.

5. Marlinda bought 32 inches of butcher paper for her project. She used $15\frac{1}{4}$ inches. How much butcher paper did she have left?

_____

6. Ingrid planted a garden. In the garden $\frac{1}{2}$ of the rows are tomatoes, $\frac{1}{4}$ of the rows are green beans, and the rest of the rows are lettuce. What fraction of the rows in the garden are lettuce?

_____

Rename each fraction as a mixed number.

7. $\frac{13}{5}$ = _____

8. $\frac{26}{12}$ = _____

9. $\frac{19}{2}$ = _____

10. $\frac{15}{4}$ = _____

Name _____

Multiply Fractions and Whole Numbers

Write the number sentence each model represents.

1.

2.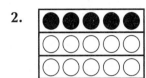

3.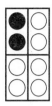

4.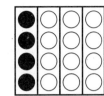

_____   _____   _____   _____

5.

6.

7.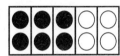

8.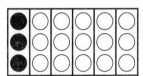

_____   _____   _____   _____

9.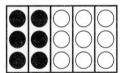

10.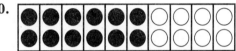

_____   _____

Find the product.

11. $\frac{1}{6} \times 18 =$ _____

12. $\frac{1}{7} \times 21 =$ _____

13. $\frac{1}{4} \times 16 =$ _____

14. $\frac{3}{8} \times 24 =$ _____

15. $\frac{2}{7} \times 14 =$ _____

16. $\frac{5}{8} \times 24 =$ _____

17. $12 \times \frac{3}{4} =$ _____

18. $24 \times \frac{5}{6} =$ _____

19. $18 \times \frac{7}{9} =$ _____

Mixed Review

20. Write $\frac{75}{100}$ in simplest form.

21. Round 65.0798 to the nearest tenth.

_____   _____

22. $6.571 + 3.1$

23. $17.012 - 5.1$

_____   _____

Multiply a Fraction by a Fraction

Find the product. Write it in simplest form.

1. $\dfrac{1}{3} \times \dfrac{1}{5}$

2. $\dfrac{2}{5} \times \dfrac{1}{4}$

3. $\dfrac{2}{3} \times \dfrac{1}{2}$

4. $\dfrac{5}{6} \times \dfrac{2}{3}$

_____   _____   _____   _____

5. $\dfrac{1}{6} \times \dfrac{1}{3}$

6. $\dfrac{2}{3} \times \dfrac{3}{5}$

7. $\dfrac{1}{4} \times \dfrac{2}{7}$

8. $\dfrac{4}{5} \times \dfrac{3}{8}$

_____   _____   _____   _____

9. $\dfrac{1}{6} \times \dfrac{7}{8}$

10. $\dfrac{3}{7} \times \dfrac{5}{8}$

11. $\dfrac{11}{12} \times \dfrac{4}{9}$

12. $\dfrac{7}{9} \times \dfrac{5}{6}$

_____   _____   _____   _____

Write the number sentence each model represents.

13.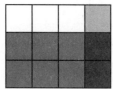

14.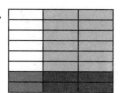

15.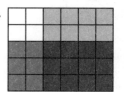

_____   _____   _____

Mixed Review

16. $\begin{array}{r} 348.9 \\ \times\ \ 7.7 \\ \hline \end{array}$

17. $\begin{array}{r} 534.26 \\ \times\ 3.4 \\ \hline \end{array}$

18. $\begin{array}{r} 58,679 \\ -17,382 \\ \hline \end{array}$

19. $\begin{array}{r} 7.8747 \\ -0.9912 \\ \hline \end{array}$

20. $6\overline{)432.6}$

21. $195\overline{)17,643.6}$

22. $2.72\overline{)0.056032}$

Multiply Fractions and Mixed Numbers

Find the product. Draw fraction squares as needed.

1. $\frac{2}{5} \times 1\frac{1}{3}$

2. $\frac{2}{3} \times 2\frac{1}{4}$

3. $\frac{3}{4} \times 3\frac{2}{3}$

_____ _____ _____

4. $\frac{1}{3} \times 2\frac{1}{4}$

5. $\frac{1}{6} \times 3\frac{1}{2}$

6. $\frac{2}{3} \times 1\frac{1}{2}$

_____ _____ _____

7. $\frac{5}{6} \times 1\frac{2}{3}$

8. $\frac{3}{4} \times 2\frac{4}{5}$

9. $\frac{1}{3} \times 3\frac{2}{5}$

_____ _____ _____

10. $\frac{2}{3} \times 2\frac{2}{3}$

11. $\frac{1}{2} \times 3\frac{5}{6}$

12. $\frac{3}{5} \times 1\frac{3}{4}$

_____ _____ _____

Mixed Review

13. $56,346$
     $-18,675$

14. $534,127$
     $- 5,621$

15. $836,142$
     $- 1,986$

16. $72,839$
     $+ 45,615$

17. $2,586.50$
     $+1,475.61$

18. $3,451.04$
     $+ 2,194.60$

19. $4,536.70$
     $+ 2,549.31$

20. 35.4849
     $- 32.0792$

Multiply with Mixed Numbers

Complete each problem. Show how to simplify before you multiply.

1. $3\frac{1}{2} \times 2\frac{2}{7}$

2. $1\frac{1}{5} \times 3\frac{3}{4}$

3. $1\frac{1}{4} \times 1\frac{1}{3}$

_____   _____   _____

4. $3\frac{1}{3} \times 2\frac{1}{4}$

5. $1\frac{1}{4} \times 1\frac{1}{5}$

6. $1\frac{2}{7} \times 1\frac{1}{6}$

_____   _____   _____

Multiply. Write the answer in simplest form.

7. $\frac{1}{2} \times 25$

8. $1\frac{1}{4} \times \frac{3}{4}$

9. $3\frac{1}{2} \times 5\frac{1}{2}$

_____   _____   _____

10. $\frac{3}{6} \times 12$

11. $3\frac{1}{4} \times \frac{1}{6} \times \frac{2}{3}$

12. $1\frac{1}{5} \times \frac{1}{4} \times 2\frac{1}{2}$

_____   _____   _____

Find the missing digit.

13. $\frac{1}{3} \times \frac{n}{8} = \frac{5}{24}$

14. $3 \times \frac{2}{n} = \frac{6}{7}$

15. $2\frac{n}{6} \times \frac{1}{8} = \frac{13}{48}$

_____   _____   _____

Mixed Review

16. 326
    $\times\ 12$

17. 475
    $\times\ 38$

18. 396
    $\times\ \ 7$

19. 491
    $\times\ 67$

Add $\frac{2}{5}$ to each number.

20. $\frac{3}{5}$

21. $\frac{7}{5}$

22. $\frac{8}{10}$

_____   _____   _____

23. $\frac{9}{2}$

24. $2\frac{1}{5}$

25. 2.4

_____   _____   _____

Problem Solving Skill

Sequence and Prioritize Information

Sequence and prioritize information to solve.

1. Julie took $100.00 to the store. She spent $15.00 on fruit, 3 times that much on meat, and $24.45 less on vegetables than she spent on meat. How much change did Julie have?

   _____

2. Mrs. Brown's Girl Scout troop had a car wash to earn some funds. They saved $\frac{1}{6}$ of the money. They used $\frac{1}{2}$ of the remaining money to go horse-back riding. They then had $100.00 left. How much did they initially make washing cars?

   _____

3. The school's track team ran the 220 relay in 7 minutes 46 seconds at their first track meet. The next meet, their time was 42 seconds shorter. At the next, their improvement was twice as great. What was their total running time at the last meet?

   _____

4. Sam's birthday is 186 days after Jim's birthday. Susan's is 24 days after Jim's. Sam was born on September 6th. What day was Susan born on if it wasn't a leap year?

   _____

Mixed Review

5.	6.	7.	8.
2.35 × 7	8.64 × 3	4.05 × 6	6.42 × 8

9.	10.	11.	12.
6.34 −0.09	8.36 +2.95	1.07 −0.09	5.9 −0.16

Write the least common multiple (LCM).

13. 6 and 12   14. 7 and 20   15. 4 and 19

_____   _____   _____

Name _____

Divide Fractions

Write a number sentence for each model.

1.

| $\frac{1}{8}$ | $\frac{1}{8}$ | $\frac{1}{8}$ | $\frac{1}{8}$ | $\frac{1}{8}$ |

| $\frac{1}{8}$ | $\rightarrow$ | $\rightarrow$ | $\rightarrow$ | $\rightarrow$ |

_____

2.

| 1 | 1 |

| $\frac{1}{4}$ | $\rightarrow$ | $\rightarrow$ | $\rightarrow$ | $\rightarrow$ | $\rightarrow$ | $\rightarrow$ | $\rightarrow$ |

_____

3.

| $\frac{1}{2}$ |

| $\frac{1}{10}$ | $\rightarrow$ | $\rightarrow$ | $\rightarrow$ | $\rightarrow$ |

_____

Use fraction bars to find the quotient.

4.

| $\frac{1}{10}$ | $\frac{1}{10}$ | $\frac{1}{10}$ | $\frac{1}{10}$ | $\frac{1}{10}$ | $\frac{1}{10}$ | $\frac{1}{10}$ | $\frac{1}{10}$ |

| $\frac{1}{5}$ | $\frac{1}{5}$ |

$\frac{8}{10} \div \frac{2}{5} = $ _____

5.

| $\frac{1}{8}$ | $\frac{1}{8}$ | $\frac{1}{8}$ | $\frac{1}{8}$ | $\frac{1}{8}$ | $\frac{1}{8}$ | $\frac{1}{8}$ |

| $\frac{1}{8}$ |

$\frac{7}{8} \div \frac{1}{8} = $ _____

6.

| 1 | 1 | 1 |

| $\frac{1}{3}$ |

$3 \div \frac{1}{3} = $ _____

7.

| 1 | 1 |

| $\frac{1}{2}$ |

$2 \div \frac{1}{2} = $ _____

8.

| $\frac{1}{10}$ | $\frac{1}{10}$ | $\frac{1}{10}$ | $\frac{1}{10}$ | $\frac{1}{10}$ | $\frac{1}{10}$ | $\frac{1}{10}$ | $\frac{1}{10}$ | $\frac{1}{10}$ |

| $\frac{1}{10}$ | $\frac{1}{10}$ | $\frac{1}{10}$ |

$\frac{9}{10} \div \frac{3}{10} = $ _____

9.

| 1 | 1 |

| $\frac{1}{5}$ | $\frac{1}{5}$ |

$2 \div \frac{2}{5} = $ _____

10.

| $\frac{1}{3}$ | $\frac{1}{3}$ |

| $\frac{1}{9}$ | $\frac{1}{9}$ |

$\frac{2}{3} \div \frac{2}{9} = $ _____

11.

| $\frac{1}{5}$ | $\frac{1}{5}$ |

| $\frac{1}{10}$ | $\frac{1}{10}$ |

$\frac{2}{5} \div \frac{2}{10} = $ _____

12.

| $\frac{1}{7}$ | $\frac{1}{7}$ | $\frac{1}{7}$ | $\frac{1}{7}$ | $\frac{1}{7}$ |

| $\frac{1}{7}$ |

$\frac{5}{7} \div \frac{1}{7} = $ _____

Mixed Review

13. Write two fractions equivalent to $\frac{5}{8}$.

_____

14. $\frac{3}{8} + \frac{1}{4}$

_____

15. $5\frac{3}{4} - 1\frac{2}{3}$

_____

Name _____

Reciprocals

Are the two numbers reciprocals? Write *yes* or *no*.

1. $3\frac{1}{3}$ and $\frac{3}{10}$

2. $\frac{1}{2}$ and $\frac{1}{2}$

3. $\frac{3}{4}$ and 4

4. 12 and $\frac{1}{12}$

_____ _____ _____ _____

Write the reciprocal of each number.

5. $\frac{9}{2}$

6. 15

7. $2\frac{3}{7}$

8. $\frac{1}{10}$

9. $\frac{3}{5}$

_____ _____ _____ _____ _____

10. $2\frac{1}{5}$

11. 4

12. $\frac{6}{7}$

13. $\frac{1}{9}$

14. $\frac{15}{4}$

_____ _____ _____ _____ _____

Algebra. Find the value of *n*.

15. $\frac{2}{n} \times \frac{5}{2} = 1$

16. $3 \times \frac{n}{3} = 1$

17. $1\frac{1}{2} \times \frac{n}{3} = 1$

18. $n \times \frac{1}{9} = 1$

_____ _____ _____ _____

Multiply. Use the Associative and Commutative Properties of Multiplication to help you.

19. $\frac{4}{7} \times \frac{3}{8} \times \frac{7}{4}$

20. $5 \times \frac{2}{3} \times \frac{1}{5} \times 12$

21. $\frac{3}{7} \times \frac{1}{8} \times 12 \times \frac{7}{3}$

_____ _____ _____

Mixed Review

Find the sum or difference. Write it in simplest form.

22. $\frac{7}{9} - \frac{5}{9}$

23. $\frac{3}{5} + \frac{1}{6}$

24. $1\frac{3}{8} + 2\frac{5}{8}$

25. $5\frac{9}{10} - 3\frac{1}{3}$

_____ _____ _____ _____

Divide.

26. $0.3)\overline{72.417}$

27. $28)\overline{4,319}$

28. $2.71)\overline{1.7615}$

29. $4,611)\overline{7,715}$

Divide Whole Numbers by Fractions

Use fraction bars, patterns, or reciprocals to divide.

1. $3 \div \frac{1}{2}$

2. $3 \div \frac{3}{8}$

3. $2 \div \frac{4}{10}$

4. $2 \div \frac{1}{4}$

_____ _____ _____ _____

Divide.

5. $8 \div \frac{4}{5}$

6. $3 \div \frac{2}{3}$

7. $10 \div \frac{5}{7}$

8. $5 \div \frac{3}{8}$

_____ _____ _____ _____

9. $12 \div \frac{2}{5}$

10. $8 \div \frac{1}{9}$

11. $9 \div \frac{3}{7}$

12. $8 \div \frac{5}{6}$

_____ _____ _____ _____

Find the missing number.

13. $7 \div \frac{6}{7} =$ _____

14. $\blacksquare \div \frac{3}{4} = 6$ _____

15. $3 \div \frac{\blacksquare}{9} = 5\frac{2}{5}$ _____

16. How many three-fourths are in 12? _____

17. How many two-sevenths are in 2? _____

18. How many one-fourths are in 9? _____

Mixed Review

Find the sum or difference. Write it in simplest form.

19. $\frac{1}{9} + \frac{5}{9}$

20. $\frac{3}{4} - \frac{1}{6}$

21. $3\frac{5}{7} - 2\frac{4}{7}$

22. $4\frac{2}{3} + \frac{5}{9}$

_____ _____ _____ _____

Write each fraction as a decimal.

23. $\frac{7}{50}$

24. $\frac{19}{25}$

25. $\frac{49}{125}$

26. $\frac{390}{400}$

_____ _____ _____ _____

Divide Fractions

Write a division sentence for each model.

1.
| $\frac{1}{9}$ | $\frac{1}{9}$ | $\frac{1}{9}$ | $\frac{1}{9}$ | $\frac{1}{9}$ | $\frac{1}{9}$ |

| $\frac{1}{9}$ | $\frac{1}{9}$ |

2.
| $\frac{1}{4}$ | $\frac{1}{4}$ | $\frac{1}{4}$ |

| $\frac{1}{8}$ |

3.
| 1 | $\frac{1}{2}$ |

| $\frac{1}{6}$ |

_____   _____   _____

Use reciprocals to write a multiplication problem for each division problem.

4. $\frac{5}{8} \div \frac{1}{4}$

5. $\frac{7}{9} \div \frac{1}{9}$

6. $\frac{7}{10} \div \frac{1}{5}$

7. $\frac{4}{5} \div 2$

_____   _____   _____   _____

Divide. Write the answer in simplest form.

8. $\frac{4}{5} \div \frac{8}{15}$

9. $\frac{7}{10} \div \frac{1}{2}$

10. $\frac{5}{6} \div \frac{1}{2}$

11. $\frac{6}{15} \div \frac{1}{5}$

_____   _____   _____   _____

12. $\frac{1}{6} \div \frac{2}{3}$

13. $\frac{7}{9} \div \frac{2}{3}$

14. $\frac{9}{10} \div \frac{2}{5}$

15. $\frac{9}{20} \div \frac{3}{4}$

_____   _____   _____   _____

16. $\frac{5}{8} \div \frac{5}{16}$

17. $\frac{5}{6} \div \frac{2}{3}$

18. $\frac{12}{21} \div \frac{4}{7}$

19. $\frac{5}{8} \div \frac{3}{4}$

_____   _____   _____   _____

Mixed Review

Write the common factors for each pair of numbers.

20. 30, 40

21. 18, 28

22. 12, 42

23. 15, 30

_____   _____   _____   _____

Write the greatest common factor for each pair of numbers.

24. 9, 18

25. 22, 24

26. 25, 30

27. 14, 49

_____   _____   _____   _____

Problem Solving Strategy

Solve a Simpler Problem

Use a simpler problem to solve.

The Robinsons drove for 4,000 miles during their vacation. This was $\frac{4}{5}$ the distance the Jones family drove during their vacation. The Edwards family did not drive, but flew 6,000 miles to their vacation spot. The Bowie family traveled $\frac{1}{2}$ of the distance of the Edwards family.

1. What equation can you write to find n if n equals the number of miles the Jones family drove?

   _____

2. Look at Problem 1. What is a simpler equation you could write? How many miles did the Jones family drive?

   _____

3. How many miles did the Bowie family drive?

   _____

   _____

   _____

4. How many more miles did the Robinson family drive than the Bowie family?

   _____

   _____

Mixed Review

5. John started exercising at 4:30 P.M. and ended at 6:15 P.M. How long did he spend exercising?

   _____

6. Solve.

   $3,000 \div \frac{3}{4}$

   _____

7. Solve.

   $34,532 - 21,412$

   _____

8. Mary wants to put a border around her picture. The picture is 6 inches wide and 5 inches high. How much border does she need to go around the picture?

   _____

Integers

Write an integer to represent each situation.

1. 15 steps behind

2. 10 days ahead of schedule

3. a gain of 35 yards

_____

_____

_____

4. 14 days after school started

5. 20 minutes until arrival time

6. a $75.00 withdrawal from the bank

_____

_____

_____

Write the opposite of each integer.

7. $^-54$ _____

8. $^-36$ _____

9. $^+3$ _____

10. $^+14$ _____

11. $^-2$ _____

12. $^+289$ _____

13. $^+3,540$ _____

14. $^-2,560$ _____

Name each integer's absolute value.

15. $|^+36|$

16. $|^-230|$

17. $|^-1,003|$

18. $|^+478|$

_____

_____

_____

_____

19. $|^-29|$

20. $|^+3,660|$

21. $|^+496|$

22. $|^-2|$

_____

_____

_____

_____

Mixed Review

23. Identify the addition property shown. $67 + 4 = 4 + 67$

24. Find n and identify the multiplication property shown. $134 \times n = 0$

_____

_____

Solve for n.

25. $76 \times 8,954 = n$

26. $3.66 \times 0.56 = n$

_____

_____

27. $34 \times n = 306$

28. $96 \div n = 8$

_____

_____

Compare and Order Integers

Compare. Write $<$, $>$, or $=$ in each $\bigcirc$.

1. $^-17 \bigcirc ^-16$ **2.** $^-10 \bigcirc ^+3$ **3.** $^-5 \bigcirc ^-7$ **4.** $^+3 \bigcirc ^-5$

Draw a number line to order each set of integers from greatest to least.

5. ⟵————————⟶

$^+3, ^-4, ^-1, 0$

_____

6. ⟵————————⟶

$^+4, ^-2, ^+5, ^-1$

_____

7. ⟵————————⟶

$^+10, ^+4, ^-9, ^+2$

_____

8. ⟵————————⟶

$^-7, ^+2, ^-6, ^+6$

_____

Algebra Name the integer that is 1 less.

9. $^-5$ **10.** $^+10$ **11.** $^-13$ **12.** $^+6$ **13.** $^-7$

_____   _____   _____   _____   _____

Algebra Name the integer that is 1 more.

14. 0 **15.** $^-9$ **16.** $^+8$ **17.** $^-5$ **18.** $^-1$

_____   _____   _____   _____   _____

Mixed Review

Order the fractions from least to greatest.

19. $\frac{1}{2}, \frac{1}{5}, \frac{3}{4}$ _____

20. $\frac{5}{6}, \frac{1}{3}, \frac{3}{8}$ _____

21. $\frac{3}{4}, \frac{3}{6}, \frac{3}{5}$ _____

22. $\frac{2}{5}, \frac{1}{4}, \frac{2}{3}$ _____

Write the sum or difference.

23. $\begin{array}{r} 284.03 \\ -\ 192.91 \\ \hline \end{array}$ **24.** $\begin{array}{r} 137.7 \\ +\ 23.62 \\ \hline \end{array}$ **25.** $\begin{array}{r} 457.6 \\ -\ 18.78 \\ \hline \end{array}$ **26.** $\begin{array}{r} 637.09 \\ -\ 138.17 \\ \hline \end{array}$

Add Integers

Write the addition number sentence modeled.

1.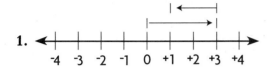

_____

2.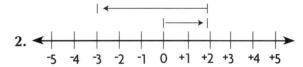

_____

3.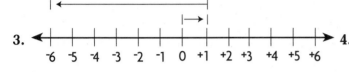

_____

4.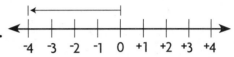

_____

Find each sum.

5. $^+7 + ^-3$

_____

6. $^-6 + ^-4$

_____

7. $^+10 + ^-3$

_____

8. $^-4 + ^-3$

_____

9. $^-7 + ^+2$

_____

10. $^-3 + ^-2$

_____

11. $^+8 + ^-8$

_____

12. $^-6 + 0$

_____

13. $^-6 + ^+8$

_____

14. $^-3 + ^+2 + ^-5$

_____

15. $^-4 + ^-3 + ^-5$

_____

16. $^+7 + ^-3 + ^-3$

_____

Reasoning Without adding, tell whether the sum will be
negative, *positive*, or *zero*.

17. $^+39 + ^-3$

_____

18. $^+3 + ^-20$

_____

19. $^+420 + ^-50$

_____

20. $^+352 + ^-352$

_____

21. $^-42 + ^+51$

_____

22. $^+36 + ^-36$

_____

23. $^+180 + ^-360$

_____

24. $^-95 + ^+95$

_____

Mixed Review

Round to the nearest hundred.

25. 651

_____

26. 1,524

_____

27. 12,345,542

_____

28. 83,952

_____

Round to the value of the underlined digit.

29. 0.7̲34

_____

30. 2̲1.638

_____

31. 5.01̲3

_____

32. 62.8̲19

_____

Subtract Integers

Use counters to find each difference.

1. $^+7 - {}^+3$

2. $^-9 - {}^+6$

3. $^+7 - {}^+6$

4. $^-5 - {}^+6$

_____

_____

_____

_____

5. $^+10 - {}^+1$

6. $^-7 - {}^+5$

7. $^+8 - {}^+4$

8. $^-6 - {}^+2$

_____

_____

_____

_____

9. $^-8 - {}^+2$

10. $^+14 - {}^+16$

11. $^-4 - {}^+4$

12. $^+12 - {}^+11$

_____

_____

_____

_____

Algebra Complete.

13. $^-6 - {}^+7 = {}^-6 + \boxed{}$

14. $^-4 - {}^+8 = {}^-4 + \boxed{}$

15. $^-7 - {}^+9 = {}^-7 + \boxed{}$

16. $^+4 - {}^+2 = {}^+4 + \boxed{}$

17. $^-1 - {}^+3 = {}^-1 + \boxed{}$

18. $^+6 - {}^+5 = {}^+6 + \boxed{}$

19. $^+8 - {}^+5 = {}^+8 + \boxed{}$

20. $^-7 - {}^+3 = {}^-7 + \boxed{}$

21. In Minnesota, the temperature was reported to be 6°F at 6:00 a.m. After an expected cold front went through, the temperature was $^-15$°F. What was the change in temperature?

_____

Mixed Review

Solve for n.

22. $11.975 - 1.993 = n$

23. $23 \times n = 92$

24. $1\frac{1}{5} + n = 3\frac{3}{4}$

_____

_____

_____

25. $\frac{1}{3} + \frac{n}{6} = \frac{5}{6}$

26. $81 \div n = 9$

27. $n + 0.74 = 0.86$

_____

_____

_____

Subtract Integers

Draw a number line to find the difference.

1. ←————————————————→

$^-6 - {}^+3$ _____

2. ←————————————————→

$^+4 - {}^+7$ _____

3. ←————————————————→

$^-1 - {}^+8$ _____

4. ←————————————————→

$^+9 - {}^+2$ _____

Write the subtraction equation modeled.

5.

-7 ⁻6 ⁻5 ⁻4 ⁻3 ⁻2 ⁻1 0 +1 +2 +3 +4 +5 +6 +7

_____

6.

⁻8 ⁻7 ⁻6 ⁻5 ⁻4 ⁻3 ⁻2 ⁻1 0 +1 +2 +3 +4 +5 +6 +7 +8

_____

Find each difference.

7. $^+17 - {}^+3$

8. $^-8 - 0$

9. $^-2 - {}^+8$

10. $^-9 - {}^+7$

_____ _____ _____ _____

11. $^+15 - {}^+4$

12. $^-6 - {}^+7$

13. $^+28 - {}^+2$

14. $^-7 - {}^+5$

_____ _____ _____ _____

Algebra Complete.

15. $^-7 - {}^+4 = {}^-7 + \square$

16. $^-3 - {}^+6 = {}^-3 + \square$

17. $^-2 - {}^+5 = {}^-2 + \square$

18. $^+1 - {}^+8 = {}^+1 + \square$

Compare. Write $<$, $>$, or $=$ in each ◯.

19. $^-3 + {}^-6 \bigcirc {}^-3 - {}^+6$

20. $^-2 - {}^+1 \bigcirc {}^-9 + {}^+4$

21. $^-7 + {}^+5 \bigcirc {}^-2 - {}^+8$

22. $^-3 - {}^+6 \bigcirc {}^-7 + {}^+5$

Mixed Review

Write as a decimal.

23. $\dfrac{1}{4}$ _____

24. $\dfrac{1}{2}$ _____

25. $\dfrac{1}{5}$ _____

Draw a Diagram

Draw a diagram to solve.

1. Sandra opened a checking account with $200.00. She wrote a check for groceries for $95.00 and a check for clothes for $65.00. Later that week she withdrew $85.00. She balanced her checkbook and realized she had over-drawn her account. How much money did she have to take to the bank to cover her overdraft and maintain a minimum of $50.00 in the account?

_____

2. John went scuba diving and dove to a depth of 30 ft. After a few minutes he realized he had ascended 5 ft. Then he noticed the coral at the bottom so he decided to descend 12 ft. Finally, he ascended 22 ft to feed the fish before returning to the surface. At what depth did he feed the fish?

_____

3. Scott spent 8 hours driving to college. If his average speed was 55 mph, how many miles did Scott drive?

_____

4. There are 12 times as many players as coaches. There are 9 coaches. How many players are there?

_____

5. Mr. Downing went on a 100–day archaeological expedition. He traveled 15 of the days. What fraction of the days did he not travel?

_____

6. There were 63 people in a hotel. Then 7 checked out, and 3 times that number checked in. How many people are in the hotel now?

_____

Mixed Review

Write as a fraction in simplest form.

7. 0.05 _____

8. 0.29 _____

9. 0.98 _____

10. 0.14 _____

11. 0.75 _____

12 0.33 _____

Name _____

Graph Relationships

Write the ordered pairs. Then graph the ordered pairs.

1.

Input, x	10	15	20	25
Output, y	5	10	15	20

_____

2.

Input, x	6	7	8	9
Output, y	11	12	13	14

_____

3.

Input, x	10	9	8	7
Output, y	7	6	5	4

_____

4.

Input, x	2	3	4	5
Output, y	6	9	12	15

_____

5.

Length of Square's Side, x	4	5	6	7
Perimeter, y	16	20	24	28

_____

6.

Number of Quarters, x	1	2	3	4
Number of Nickels, y	5	10	15	20

_____

Use Data For 7–8, use the table.

Tickets sold, x	1	2	3	4
Money received, y	$4	$8	$12	$16

7. Write the ordered pairs. Then graph the ordered pairs.

_____

_____

8. How can you use the graph to find the amount of money 5 tickets cost?

_____

_____

_____

Mixed Review

9. If x = 22, what is the value of (x + 48)?

10. 45,679,231
+ 12,382,938

11. Find the mode of the data set: 159, 156, 159, 166, 164, 162

12. Find the mean of the data set in problem 11.

Name _____

Graph Integers on the Coordinate Plane

For 1–8, identify the ordered pair for each point.

1. Point *A*   _____
2. Point *B*   _____
3. Point *C*   _____
4. Point *D*   _____
5. Point *E*   _____
6. Point *F*   _____
7. Point *G*   _____
8. Point *H*   _____

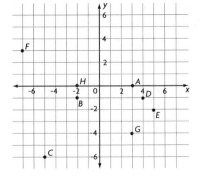

Graph and label the ordered pairs on a coordinate plane.

9. *A* $(0,{}^+7)$
10. *B* $({}^+4,0)$
11. *C* $({}^+2,{}^+6)$
12. *D* $({}^-3,{}^+6)$
13. *E* $({}^+5,{}^-3)$
14. *F* $({}^-2,{}^+7)$
15. *G* $({}^+1,{}^+6)$
16. *H* $({}^-5,{}^+6)$
17. *J* $({}^+4,{}^+6)$

For 18–23, name the ordered pair that is described.

18. Start at the origin. Move 6 units to the left and 4 units up.

19. Start at the origin. Move 4 units to the right and 4 units down.

20. Start at the origin. Move 0 units to the right and 2 units up.

21. Start at the origin. Move 3 units to the left and 0 units down.

22. Start at the origin. Move 1 unit to the left and 5 units down.

23. Start at the origin. Move 2 units to the right and 3 units up.

Mixed Review

24. 348×25

25. $30.8 - 16.925$

26. $7.000 \div 8$

27. $1\frac{3}{4} + 2\frac{3}{8}$

28. $3\frac{1}{6} - 1\frac{2}{3}$

29. $1.87 + 32.6 + 0.555$

Use an Equation to Graph

Use a rule to complete the table. Then write the equation.

1.

Feet, x	2	4	6	8
Toes, y	10	20	30	

_____

2.

Grapes, x	10	14	16	18
Oranges, y	6	10	12	

_____

3.

Bikes, x	3	4	5	6
Wheels, y	6	8	10	

_____

4.

Triangles, x	2	3	4	5
Sides, y	6	9	12	

_____

Use a rule to complete the table, write the ordered pairs, and then make a graph.

5.

x	5	4	3	2	1
y	3	2	1		

6.

x	3	6	9	12	15
y	1	2	3		

7.

x	$^-6$	$^-7$	$^-8$	$^-9$	$^-10$
y	$^-2$	$^-3$	$^-4$		

8.

x	$^-2$	$^-3$	$^-4$	$^-5$	$^-6$
y	$^-5$	$^-6$	$^-7$		

Use each equation to make a table with at least 4 ordered pairs. Then graph.

9. $y = x + 5$

10. $y = 3x + {}^-2$

11. $y = 2x$

12. $y = {}^-4 + x$

13. $y = x - 0$

14. $y = {}^-5 + x$

15. $y = 3x$

16. $y = x - 6$

Mixed Review

17. $789,990 - 543,834 =$ _____

18. $20.08 \times 324 =$ _____

19. Round to the nearest ten thousand. 45,213,021

_____

20. Find the range for this set of data.
12, 42, 24, 53, 12, 17, 34

_____

Problem Solving Skill: Relevant or Irrelevant Information

For 1–2, use the map. Tell the relevant information and solve.

1. The park and the stadium have the same y-coordinate. The x-coordinate of the park is 2 less than the police station's y-coordinate. The firehouse is 4 units right and 3 units down from the police station. Where is the park?

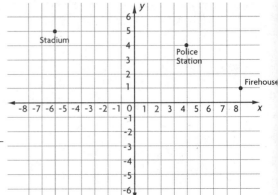

_____

2. The soccer field was built before the stadium. It is south of the park and east of the stadium. If you go 3 units west of the police station, you will find the soccer field. Where is the soccer field?

_____

Lara skated to the playground, which is 3 blocks north of her house. Then she turned west and skated 4 blocks to her friend's house. Before going home, she stopped at the store, which is 3 blocks south of her friend's house. She then returned home. How many blocks did she skate?

3. Which information is relevant to solving the problem?

   A Lara skated to the playground.

   B Her friend lives west of the playground.

   C The store is 3 blocks south of Lara's friend's house.

   D The playground is north of Lara's house.

4. Which question cannot be answered with the given information?

   F How far is Lara's house from the store?

   G In which direction did Lara travel home from the store?

   H Could Lara have taken a shorter route?

   J How far is the playground from the store?

5. In the number 268,743, how many times greater than the 3 is the 6?

_____

6. Write the next 4 letters in this sequence: A, B, Z, Y, C, D, . . .

_____

Lines and Angles

For 1–5, use the figure at the right. Name an example of each term.

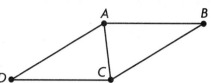

1. Angle

_____

2. Acute Angle

_____

3. Obtuse Angle

_____

4. Point

_____

5. Line Segment

_____

Draw and label a figure for each.

6. $\overline{AB}$ 7. Point C 8. $\overrightarrow{BG}$

For 9–11, use the figure.

9. Name a line segment parallel to $\overline{AB}$.

_____

10. Name a line segment that intersects $\overline{DA}$.

_____

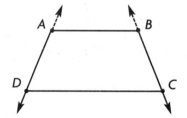

11. Name two line segments that are not parallel.

_____

Mixed Review

12. Solve for n.

$$\frac{600}{n} = 20$$

13. What is $\frac{1}{3}$ of 270?

_____   _____

Measure and Draw Angles

1. The unit used to measure an angle is called
   a _____.

2. A _____ is a tool for measuring
   the size of the opening of an angle.

Use a protractor to measure and classify each angle.

3.

_____

4.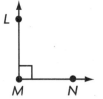

_____

5.

_____

6.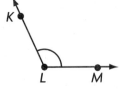

_____

7.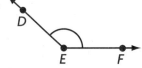

_____

8.

_____

Mixed Review

Solve.

9. $55\overline{)555{,}555}$

10. 2^8

11. 3^5

12. $3\overline{)4{,}527}$

_____ _____ _____ _____

13. 325
   $\times\ 12$

14. 673
   $\times\ 25$

15. 518
   $\times\ 42$

16. 236
   $\times\ 18$

17. 639
   $\times\ 48$

Name _____

Angles and Polygons

1. A _____ is a closed plane figure formed by three or more line segments.

2. If all the sides have equal length and the angles measure the same, the figure is a _____.

Name each polygon and tell if it is *regular* or *not regular*.

3.

4.

5.

6.

_____ _____ _____ _____

_____ _____ _____ _____

Use dot paper to draw an example of each.

7. regular hexagon

8. regular quadrilateral

9. octagon that is not regular

10. regular triangle

Find the unknown angle measure.

11.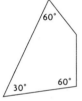

12.

13.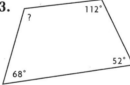

14.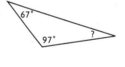

_____ _____ _____ _____

Find the pattern. Then write a rule. Use your rule to draw the next figure in the pattern.

15. △ △△△ △△ △△△△ △△△

16.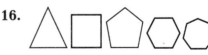

_____ _____

Mixed Review

17. 7,777
   ×   77

18. What is the square root of 256?

19. 12)82,432

20. What is 4^4?

_____ _____ _____ _____

Circles

Vocabulary

Write the correct letter from Column 2.

Column 1   Column 2

1. chord   ——   **a.** a tool for constructing circles

2. diameter   ——   **b.** a line segment that connects the center with
                                        a point on the circle

3. circle   ——   **c.** a line segment that connects any two points
                                        on the circle

4. radius   ——   **d.** a closed figure with all points on the figure
                                        the same distance from the center point.

5. compass   ——   **e.** a chord that passes through the center of
                                        the circle

For 6–7, use circle C.

6. If $\overline{AC}$ is 6 in. long, how   **7.** If $\overline{AC}$ is 6 in. long, how
long is $\overline{CE}$?   long is $\overline{AD}$?

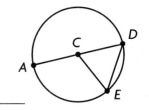

_____   _____

Use a compass to draw each circle. Draw the radius and the
diameter, and label the measurements.

8. radius = _____   **9.** radius = 4 cm   **10.** radius = _____

diameter = 5 cm   diameter = _____   diameter = 6 cm

Mixed Review

11.   436   **12.** 26)2,704   **13.** 5^2 **14.** 2^5
        × 85

_____   _____   _____   _____

Congruent and Similar Figures

Write *similar*, *congruent*, or *neither* to describe each pair.

1.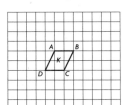

2.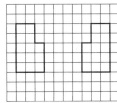

3.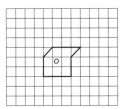

_____   _____   _____

For 4–6, use the figures below.

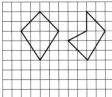 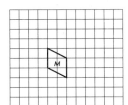  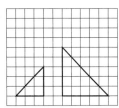

4. Write the letter of the figure that is neither congruent nor similar to Figure *K*.

_____

5. Write the letter of the figure that is similar but not congruent to Figure *K*.

_____

6. Write the letter of the figure that is congruent to Figure *K*.

_____

Mixed Review

7. 6.97
   +3.1
   _____

8. 8.43
   −7.96
   _____

9. 5.02
   +6.09
   _____

10. 4.85
   −1.94
   _____

11. 5.93
   −3.59
   _____

Symmetric Figures

Draw the lines of symmetry for each figure. Tell whether each
figure has rotational symmetry. Write *yes* or *no*.

1.

_____

2.

_____

3.

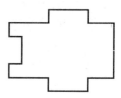

_____

4.

_____

5.

_____

6.

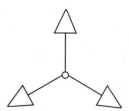

_____

Each figure has rotational symmetry. Tell the fraction and angle
measure of each turn.

7.

_____

8

_____

9.

_____

Mixed Review

10. Find the next number in the
sequence: 1, 3, 6, 10, 15, . . .

_____

11. Find the change from a $20 bill
for purchases totaling $17.21.

_____

12. What is $\frac{2}{3}$ of 90?

13. Dave has saved $65.50 for a radio
that costs $74.98 including tax.
How much more does he need to
save?

_____

_____

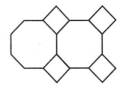

Problem Solving Strategy: Find a Pattern

Find a pattern to solve. Describe the pattern.

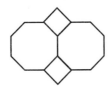

| Step 1 | Step 2 | Step 3 | Step 4 |

1. What shape or shapes would be added at Step 6?

_____

2. What shape or shapes would be added at Step 9?

_____

1 red, 2 yellow,   4 blue,   2 red,   4 yellow,   _____, _____
                                                    (Step 6)   (Step 7)

3. What color will the blocks in Step 6 be?

_____

4. How many blocks will be in Step 6?

_____

5. What color blocks will be added at Step 7?

_____

6. How many blocks will be added at Step 9?

_____

7. What is the next number in this pattern? 3, 4, 7, 8, 11, . . . ?

_____

8.

What is shape of the 16th bead?

_____

Mixed Review

Solve.

9. 8,535
     ×   9

10. A triangle has two angles measuring 45° and 61°. What is the third angle?

11. $11\overline{)99{,}341}$

_____   _____   _____

Triangles

Classify each triangle. Write *isosceles, scalene,* or *equilateral.*

1. 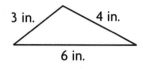 3 in. 4 in. 6 in.

2. 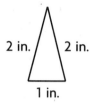 2 in. 2 in. 1 in.

3. 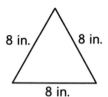 8 in. 8 in. 8 in.

_____   _____   _____

Classify each triangle. Write *right, acute,* or *obtuse.*

4. 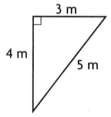 3 m 4 m 5 m

5. 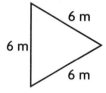 6 m 6 m 6 m

6. 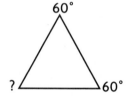 6 m 2 m 5 m

_____   _____   _____

Find the unknown angle measure.

7. 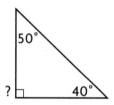 50° ? 40°

8. 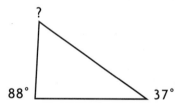 ? 88° 37°

9. 60° ? 60°

_____   _____   _____

Use a protractor and ruler to draw triangle *ABC* according to the given measurements. Classify the triangle by its sides and by its angles. Then find the measure of the third angle.

10. $\angle A = 65°$, $\angle C = 65°$, $\overline{AC} = 4$ in.

11. $\angle C = 50°$, $\angle B = 20°$, $\overline{CB} = 2.5$ in.

_____   _____

Mixed Review

Add or subtract. Write the answer in simplest form.

12. $\frac{1}{2}$
$+ \frac{3}{4}$

13. $\frac{3}{4}$
$- \frac{1}{8}$

14. $1\frac{1}{2}$
$+ \frac{3}{8}$

15. $3\frac{1}{6}$
$- \frac{5}{6}$

16. $2\frac{1}{8}$
$+ \frac{5}{6}$

17. $\frac{3}{10}$
$+ \frac{5}{8}$

Quadrilaterals

Vocabulary

Write the correct letter from Column 2.

Column 1   **Column 2**

_____ 1. has 4 congruent sides and 2 pairs of
           congruent angles   **a.** quadrilateral

_____ 2. has 2 pairs of congruent and parallel   **b.** trapezoid
           sides
                                                               c. parallelogram
_____ 3. has 4 sides of any length and 4 angles of
           any size   **d.** rhombus

_____ 4. has only 1 pair of parallel sides

Draw and classify each quadrilateral described.

5. adjacent sides not equal; 2 pairs   6. opposite sides not parallel;
   of congruent sides; 4 right angles   angles not equal

   _____   _____

7. a parallelogram with congruent   8. equal angles; 4 congruent sides
   sides

   _____   _____

9. 2 pairs of parallel sides; 2 pairs of   10. angles not equal; only one pair of
   equal angles   parallel sides

   _____   _____

Mixed Review

11. 17^3 12. $0.25\overline{)16.84}$ 13. $\begin{array}{r} 336.98 \\ \times\ \ \ \ 1.8 \\ \hline \end{array}$ 14. $\frac{6}{7} + \frac{7}{5}$

_____   _____   _____   _____

Algebra: Transformations

Vocabulary

Complete.

1. When you move a figure to show a translation, reflection,

or rotation, it is called a _____ .

Graph the triangle with vertices $(^+2,^+4)$, $(^+2,^+6)$, and $(^+6,^+4)$.
Then transform the triangle to the new given vertices. Write
translation, reflection, or *rotation* to describe the move.

2. $(^-2,^+4)$, $(^-2,^+6)$, $(^-6,^+4)$

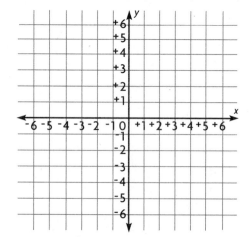

3. $(^+2,^+4)$, $(^+4,^+4)$, $(^+2,0)$

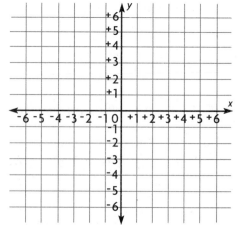

4. $(^-6,^-4)$, $(^-6,^-2)$, $(^-2,^-4)$

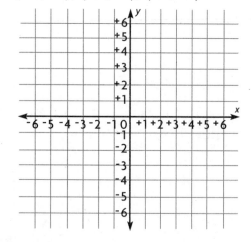

5. $(^+2,^-4)$, $(^+2,^-6)$, $(^+6,^-4)$

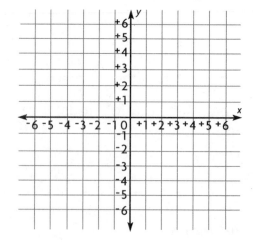

Mixed Review

6. $\begin{array}{r} 5.5 \\ \times\ 6.5 \\ \hline \end{array}$

7. $\dfrac{3}{4} - \dfrac{15}{20}$

8. $0.5\overline{)0.985}$

9. $\begin{array}{r} \$18,350.66 \\ -\ \ \ \ \ 681.08 \\ \hline \end{array}$

_____ _____ _____

Solid Figures

Vocabulary

Complete.

1. A _____ is a polyhedron that has two

   congruent faces called _____.

2. A _____ is a solid figure with

   one _____ that is a polygon and three
   or more faces that are triangles with a common vertex.

3. A _____ is a solid figure with faces that are polygons.

Classify the solid figure. Then, write the number of faces, vertices, and edges.

4.

5.

6.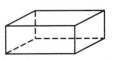

_____   _____   _____

_____   _____   _____

Draw and classify each figure described.

7. I have 1 flat circular base. I have
   1 curved surface.

8. I have a base with 8 equal sides.
   My faces are 8 triangles.

_____   _____

Mixed Review

9. Write 0.125 as
   a fraction in
   simplest form.

10. 0.393
    $\times$ 3.93

11. Write $\frac{80}{100}$ in
    simplest form.

12. $290,460.81
    +   6,387.24

_____   _____   _____   _____

Draw Solid Figures from Different Views

Use grid paper to draw each figure from the top, the side, and the front.

1. 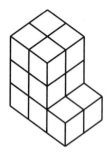 2. 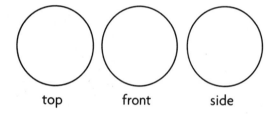 3.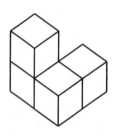

Identify the solid figure that has the given views.

4.

    top   front   side

_____

5.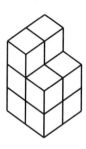

    top   front   side

_____

6.

    top   front   side

_____

7.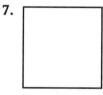

    top   front   side

_____

Mixed Review

8.   9.78
    × 21
   _____

9. Write three fractions equivalent to $\frac{3}{8}$.

10. 6^5

11.   316
   − 279
   _____

12. Solve for x.
    $4 + x = 10$

13. 7^3

Problem Solving Skill: Make Generalizations

Make generalizations to solve.

1. The Towers Dormitories at the University of Pittsburgh are three congruent prisms. If a side of Tower A is 229.5 feet high, how high is a side of Tower C?

_____

2. The World Trade Center buildings in New York City are two rectangular prisms. They both have 110 stories. One tower is 4 feet shorter than the other. Are the heights of their stories the same?

_____

3. A plane figure has 6 congruent sides. The perimeter of the figure is 96 meters. What is the length of each side?

_____

4. The distance between Youngstown and Ashville is the same as the distance between Canton and Youngstown. If it takes 2 hours to drive from Youngstown to Ashville, how long should it take to drive from Youngstown to Canton?

_____

5. Betty is cutting a rectangular cake. It measures 12 inches long by 6 inches wide. If each piece is 3 inches square, how many pieces can she cut?

_____

6. Bart and Brett are identical twins. Brendan and Britt are also identical twins. Can you find the ages of Bart and Brett? Explain.

_____

Mixed Review

7. $90\overline{)363,636}$

8. $\frac{31}{32} - \frac{1}{4}$

9. $\begin{array}{r} 363,636 \\ \times \quad 96 \\ \hline \end{array}$

10. What is 9^4?

_____   _____   _____   _____

Customary Length

Vocabulary

1. The smaller the unit, the more _____ the measurement will be.

Estimate the length in inches. Then measure to the nearest $\frac{1}{16}$ inch.

2.
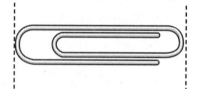

_____

3.

_____

Estimate the length in inches. Then measure to the nearest $\frac{1}{8}$ inch.

4.

_____

5.
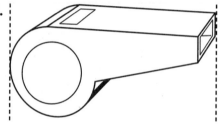

_____

Draw a line segment to the given length.

6. $1\frac{3}{4}$ inches

7. $2\frac{3}{16}$ inches

8. $3\frac{5}{16}$ inches

Mixed Review

9. Karina's art teacher gave her an $8\frac{1}{2}$-inch by 11-inch piece of paper. He told her to leave a $\frac{3}{4}$-inch margin on all 4 sides. What are the dimensions of the remaining area?

10. Elise measures her hair ribbon. It is $9\frac{2}{3}$ inches long. Mindy's hair ribbon is $9\frac{5}{8}$ inches long. Who has the longer hair ribbon? How much longer?

_____   _____

Metric Length

Estimate the length in centimeters. Measure to the nearest centimeter and then to the nearest millimeter.

1.

_____

2.

_____

3.

_____

4.

_____

Draw a line segment to the given length.

5. 4 cm 3 mm

6. 6 cm 1 mm

7. 1.4 cm

8. 8 mm

Mixed Review

9. Write <, >, or = for ◯.

   3.78 ◯ $3\frac{3}{4}$

10. What kind of triangle has a 90° angle?

_____

11. Write $\frac{6}{9}$ in simplest form.

12. Write $6\frac{1}{8}$ as a decimal.

_____

13. Would you rather buy 6 yards or 17 feet of fabric, each selling at the same price?

_____

14. What is the least common multiple of 8 and 14?

_____

Change Linear Units

Change the unit.

1. 65 cm = _____ mm   **2.** 400 cm = _____ m   **3.** 60 in. = _____ ft

4. 3 yd = _____ in.   **5.** 36 ft = _____ yd   **6.** 1,760 yd = _____ mi

Complete.

7. 7 km 8 m = 6 km ☐ m   **8.** 3 mi 27 ft = 2 mi ☐ ft   **9.** 10 ft = ☐ yd 1 ft

_____   _____   _____

Find the sum or difference.

10.   6 ft 5 in.   **11.**   9 yd 7 ft   **12.**   9 m 20 cm   **13.**   15 m 4 cm
     +3 ft 9 in.   −6 yd 8 ft   −7 m 30 cm   + 6 m 2 cm

Mixed Review

Find the product.

14.   2,345   **15.**   1,789   **16.**   3,060
     ×   16   ×   25   ×   32

Order from *least* to *greatest*.

17. $2\frac{2}{11}$, $1\frac{5}{8}$, $2\frac{1}{9}$, $1\frac{3}{7}$ **18.** $\frac{26}{3}$, $\frac{22}{4}$, $\frac{16}{5}$, $\frac{21}{3}$, $\frac{19}{2}$

_____   _____

19. Karen is counting the change in her drawer. When she gets 6 more nickels, she will have $5.00 in nickels. How many nickels does she have now?

20. The Ryan family traveled 64 miles on Friday and 60.2 miles on Saturday. The Jones family traveled 59.3 miles on Friday and 63.4 miles on Saturday. Which family traveled more miles? How many more?

_____   _____

Name _____

Customary Capacity and Weight

Change the unit.

1. 16 pt = ☐ gal   **2.** 10 c = ☐ pt   **3.** 4 qt = ☐ c   **4.** 1 gal = ☐ c

_____   _____   _____   _____

5. 32 fl oz = ☐ pt   **6.** 3 T = ☐ lb   **7.** 16 qt = ☐ gal   **8.** 8 c = ☐ fl oz

_____   _____   _____   _____

Choose the best estimate.

9. A bucket of ice cream holds _____.

   a. 1 gallon

   b. 1 cup

   c. 1 pint

11. A truck weighs _____.

   a. 300 pounds

   b. 5 tons

   c. 20 ounces

10. A coffee cup holds _____.

   a. 1 gallon

   b. 3 pints

   c. 1 cup

12. A cat weights _____.

   a. 300 pounds

   b. 16 ounces

   c. 15 pounds

Mixed Review

Find the sum, difference, or product.

13. $2\frac{3}{4} + 1\frac{1}{8}$ **14.** $3 \times \frac{2}{5}$ **15.** $\begin{array}{r} 24.06 \\ -15.59 \\ \hline \end{array}$

16. What angles are greater than 90° but less than 180°?

17. What are the prime numbers between 5 and 13?

18. If you started a bike race at 11:30 A.M. and you finished 2 hours later, what time would it be?

19. Write fourteen thousand and six tenths in standard form.

Metric Capacity and Mass

Change the unit.

1. 1.5 L = ☐ metric cups   2. 2,000 L = ☐ kL   3. 5,000 mg = ☐ g

_____   _____   _____

Choose the best estimate.

4.

mass of an apple pie is _____

a. 1 mg

b. 1 g

c. 1 kg

5.

mass of the puppy is _____

a. 2 kg

b. 2 g

c. 2 mg

6.

the cup holds _____

a. 3 L

b. 3 mL

c. 3 kL

7.

mass of a paper clip is _____

a. 1 mg

b. 1 kg

c. 1 g

Mixed Review

8. $600 \div 0.03$

_____

9. $16.48 + 3.2 = n$

_____

10. Write 16,345,107 in word form.

_____

_____

_____

11. Write 21.45 as a fraction.

_____

12. What is the sum of the angles in a triangle?

_____

13. In which place would you write the first digit of the quotient for $2.682 \div 4$?

_____

Time

Write the time for each.

1. Start: 9:00 A.M.

   Elapsed: _____

   End: 1:50 P.M.

2. Start: 7:27 A.M.

   Elapsed: 4 hr 24 min

   End: _____

3. Start: Dec 1, 10:15 P.M.

   Elapsed: 4 hr 10 min

   End: _____

4. Start: _____

   Elapsed: 16 hr 35 min

   End: March 18, 3:25 A.M.

5. Start: 12:15 P.M.

   Elapsed: _____

   End: 8:05 P.M.

6. Start: _____

   Elapsed: 6 hr 15 min

   End: 7:25 P.M.

Add or subtract.

7.   3 hr 25 min
    $+$6 hr 50 min

8.   4 hr 10 min
    $-$1 hr 30 min

9.   3 hr 1 min
    $+$5 hr 19 min

10.   9 hr 5 min
    $-$2 hr 50 min

11.   8 hr 5 min
    $+$2 hr 25 min

12.   5 hr 20 min
    $-$2 hr 45 min

13.   6 hr 3 min
    $+$6 hr 34 min

14.   7 hr 57 min
    $-$6 hr 38 min

Mixed Review

15. Bob bought 50 yards of velvet and 40 yards of denim to recover the chairs. The velvet cost $45.99 per yard and the denim cost $6.50 per yard. What was his total bill?

    _____

16. Julie bought 16 pounds of apples at $1.69 per pound. How much did Julie pay?

    _____

17. $n + 3 = 4 \times 7$

    _____

18. $5\frac{3}{8} + 6\frac{1}{4}$

    _____

Problem Solving Strategy: Make a Table

Make a table to solve.

1. The pool at the community center is open daily. The swim team occupies the pool from 6:00 A.M. until 8:30 A.M. Then there is a one-hour open swim followed by four different 45-minute swim classes. At what time is the pool available?

2. Tomás starts his activities at camp at 9:30 A.M. He has swimming for $1\frac{1}{2}$ hours, archery for 1 hour, and lunch for 30 minutes. Then he has crafts for $2\frac{1}{2}$ hours. At what time does Tomás finish crafts?

3. The Youth Symphony begins auditions at 10:00 A.M. Each student is given 10 minutes to perform. If Claudia is the 12th in line, at what time is her audition?

4. Kelly reads to children at the library. There are 3 sessions. Each lasts 45 minutes, with 30 minutes between sessions. If Kelly starts reading at 10:00 A.M., at what time does she finish?

Mixed Strategy Practice

Solve.

5. Yoma bought a 32-ounce box of raisins for $3.28. Liz paid $1.79 for a pound of raisins. Who got the better price? Explain.

6. Gil's mom has the car's oil changed every 3,000 miles. If she drives 18,000 miles per year, how many times is the oil changed each year?

7. What is the next number in the pattern? 24, 19, 14, 9, ■

8. The museum sells 3 maps for $12.99. How much is each map?

Name _____

Perimeter

Find the perimeter of each polygon.

1.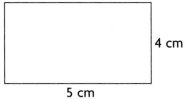
5 cm, 4 cm

2.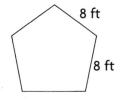
8 ft, 8 ft

3.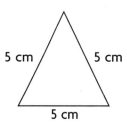
5 cm, 5 cm, 5 cm

4.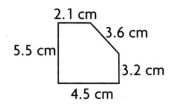
2.1 cm, 3.6 cm, 5.5 cm, 3.2 cm, 4.5 cm

5.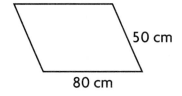
50 cm, 80 cm

6.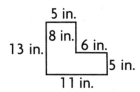
5 in., 8 in., 6 in., 13 in., 5 in., 11 in.

7.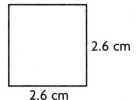
2.6 cm, 2.6 cm

8.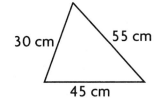
30 cm, 55 cm, 45 cm

9.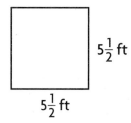
$5\frac{1}{2}$ ft, $5\frac{1}{2}$ ft

Mixed Review

10. Name the addition property used in this equation. $(9 + 1) + 3 = 9 + (1 + 3)$

11. What number's value is 100,000 less than 1,547,298?

12. Write forty-five ten-thousandths in standard form.

13. $8.9 + 0.92 + 0.095 + 8.4 + 0.9$

14. $6 \times \$1.65$

15. $16\overline{)450}$

Algebra: Circumference

For 1–6 complete the table.

	C	d	C ÷ d
1.	9.42 cm	3 cm	_____
2.	5 in.	_____	3.14
3.	4.5 ft	_____	3.14
4.	_____	7 mi	3.14
5.	12 yd	_____	3.14
6.	_____	8.5 cm	3.14

Find the circumference of a circle that has

7. a diameter of 34 in.

_____

8. a radius of 6 ft.

_____

9. a radius of 2 m.

_____

10. a diameter of 100 yd.

_____

Mixed Review

11. What is the perimeter of a square that measures 4.5 ft on one side?

_____

12. Write one hundred thirty-five ten-thousandths in standard form.

_____

13. Find the average of 1.5, 2, 2.5, and 1.

_____

14. Each player on the basketball team is required to have an average of 80 or better. 76, 85, 70, 90, 71, and 82 are the math scores of one basketball player. Find his average. Will he be able to play on the team?

_____

15. $12 \times n = 600$

_____

16. $23\overline{)658}$

_____

Algebra: Area of Squares and Rectangles

Find the area of each figure.

1.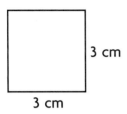

3 cm

3 cm

_____

2.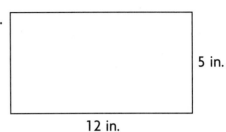

5 in.

12 in.

_____

3.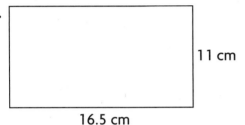

11 cm

16.5 cm

_____

4.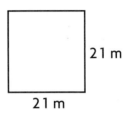

21 m

21 m

_____

Find each missing measurement.

5. $s = 3.2$ yd

$A = \blacksquare$

_____

6. $s = 5\frac{1}{2}$ in.

$A = \blacksquare$

_____

7. $s = 60$ cm

$A = \blacksquare$

_____

8. $l = 9$ m

$w = 12$ m

$A = \blacksquare$

_____

9. $l = \blacksquare$

$w = 3.1$ mi

$A = 31$ mi^2

_____

10. $l = 4.5$ ft

$w = \blacksquare$

$A = 72$ ft^2

_____

Mixed Review

11. $22\overline{)456}$

12. Name the factors of 11. Is it a prime or composite number?

_____

Relate Perimeter and Area

Use the grid below to draw rectangles for the given perimeter.
Name the length and width of the rectangle with the greatest area.
(Use whole numbers.)

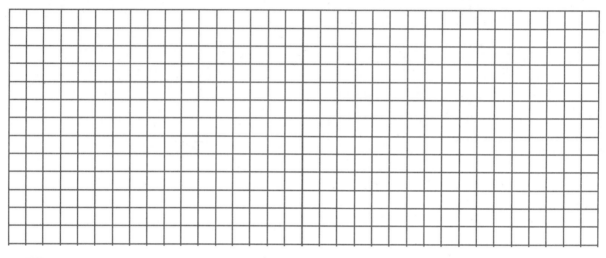

1. 50 cm   2. 34 cm   3. 12 cm

_____   _____   _____

Find the dimensions of the rectangle with the least perimeter for
the given area. (Use whole numbers.)

4. 30 cm^2 5. 12 cm^2 6. 21 cm^2

_____   _____   _____

7. 50 cm^2 8. 4 cm^2 9. 48 cm^2

_____   _____   _____

Mixed Review

10. What is the least common   11. Change $\frac{1}{20}$ to a decimal.
    multiple of 15 and 10?

_____   _____

12. $\frac{1}{3} + \frac{2}{5}$ 13. Change 42 inches to feet.

_____   _____

Algebra: Area of Triangles

Find the area of each triangle.

1.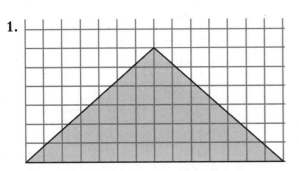

_____

2.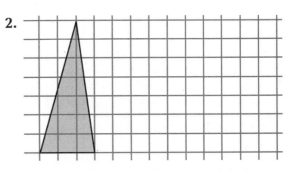

_____

Find the area of each triangle.

3. base (b) = 4 cm

   height (h) = 5 cm

   _____

4. base (b) = 12 yd

   height (h) = 12 yd

   _____

5. base (b) = 3.5 mi

   height (h) = 10 mi

   _____

6. base (b) = 10 in.

   height (h) = 4 in.

   _____

7. base (b) = 7 ft

   height (h) = 6 ft

   _____

8. base (b) = 21 cm

   height (h) = 12 cm

   _____

Find the missing measurement for each triangle.

9. base (b) = ■

   height (h) = 50 cm

   Area (A) = 800 cm^2

   _____

10. base (b) = 32 ft

    height (h) = ■

    Area (A) = 160 ft^2

    _____

11. base (b) = 4 cm

    height (h) = ■

    Area (A) = 18 cm^2

    _____

Mixed Review

12. What is the circumference of a circle that has a diameter of 8 m?

13. Is 42 a prime or composite number? What are its factors?

_____   _____

Algebra: Area of Parallelograms

Write the base and height of each figure.

1.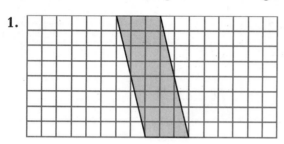

2.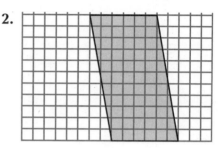

_____   _____

Find the area of each parallelogram.

3. base (b) = 3 in.

   height (h) = 6 in.

4. base (b) = 7.5 cm

   height (h) = 4 cm

_____   _____

Find the missing measurement for the parallelogram.

5. base (b) = 22.5 cm

   height (h) = 5 cm

   Area (A) = ■

6. base (b) = ■

   height (h) = 12 yd

   Area (A) = 98.4 yd^2

7. base (b) = 3.5 mi

   height (h) = ■

   Area (A) = 7.7 mi^2

_____   _____   _____

Mixed Review

8. What is the area of a triangle with a base of 5 inches and a height of 6.5 inches?

9. What is the median of this set of data? 45, 60, 34, 56, 20, 90, 34

_____   _____

10. Write a number between 1.03 and 1.10.

11. What number's value is 10,000 greater than 298,469?

_____   _____

Name _____

Area of Irregular Figures

Find the area. Each square is 1 cm².

1.

_____

2.

_____

3.

_____

4.

_____

5.

_____

6.

_____

Estimate the area. Each square is 1 cm².

7.

_____

8.

_____

9.

_____

10.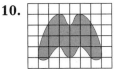

_____

11.

_____

12.

_____

Mixed Review

Find the quotient. Check by multiplying.

13. $3\overline{)1.44}$

14. $8\overline{)14.32}$

15. $4\overline{)0.56}$

Find the sum or difference. Write the answer in simplest form.

16. $\frac{5}{12} + \frac{1}{4}$

17. $\frac{6}{9} + \frac{2}{3}$

18. $\frac{2}{5} - \frac{3}{10}$

19. $\frac{7}{8} - \frac{3}{16}$

_____   _____   _____   _____

Problem Solving Strategy: Solve a Simpler Problem

Solve a simpler problem to solve.

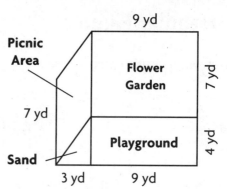

1. What is the area of the smallest section of the park?

_____

2. What is the area of the largest section of the park?

_____

3. How many square yards is the park?

_____

4. If a 2 yd by 6 yd rectangular pond were built next to the picnic section, what would the new area of the park be?

_____

Mixed Review

5. Each bottle of fertilizer covers 25 ft². How many bottles does the gardener need to fertilize the playground?

_____

6. It takes the gardener 5 minutes to mow 50 ft². How long will it take him to mow the playground?

_____

7. The sun's surface is close to 10,000°F. Its inner core may reach temperatures near 35 million degrees. The diameter of the sun is 864,000 mi. Tell whether too much or too little information was given to find the circumference of the sun.

_____

8. Nine planets revolve around the sun along oval-shaped paths. The Earth takes one year or 365 days to make one revolution. Tell whether too much or too little information was given to find the distance from the Earth to the sun.

_____

9. What is the perimeter of an equilateral triangle that has a side length of 16 cm?

_____

10. What is the area of a triangle that has a base of 4 in. and a height of 4 in.?

_____

Name _____

Nets for Solid Figures

Vocabulary

Complete.

A _____ is a two-dimensional pattern for
a three-dimensional prism or pyramid.

Match each solid figure with its net. Write a, b, c, or d.

1.   2.   3.   4.

_____   _____   _____   _____

a. 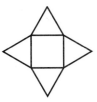   b. 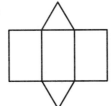   c. 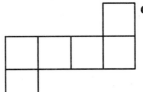   d.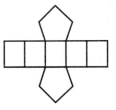

Circle the letter of the net that can be folded to make the figure.

5.   a.   b.   c.

6.   a.   b. 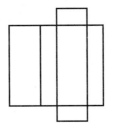   c.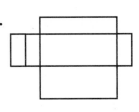

Mixed Review

7. What faces would you find in a
   net for a square pyramid?

8. Cara earns $36.75 a week for 7
   hours of babysitting. How much
   does she earn in 4 weeks? How
   much does she earn an hour?

_____   _____

_____   _____

Surface Area

Use the net to find the area of each face. Then find the surface area of each prism.

1.

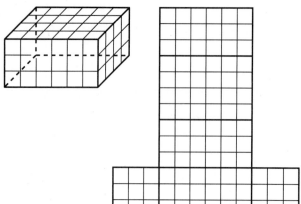

_____

2.

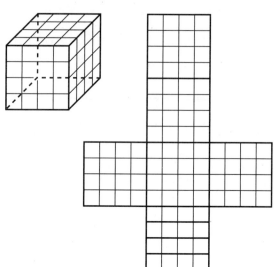

_____

For 3–4, find the surface area in cm². You may want to make the net.

3.

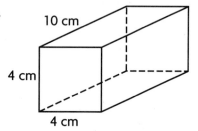

10 cm
4 cm
4 cm

_____

4.

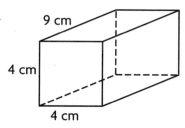

9 cm
4 cm
4 cm

_____

5. What is the surface area of a box 6 feet long, 4 feet wide, and 8 feet high?

_____

6. What is the surface area of a cube whose sides are 12 feet long?

_____

Mixed Review

7. $8 - 2\frac{3}{8}$ 8. $35.8 \div 2$

9. 3.5×4.9 10. $5.79 \div 3$

11. List all possible digits for ■.
    $5.31 < 5.■2 < 5.53$

12. Compare. Write $<$, $>$, or $=$.
    $0.532 ● 0.083$

_____

_____

Name _____

Algebra: Volume

Find the volume of each rectangular prism.

1.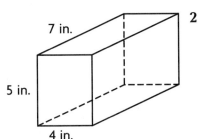
7 in.
5 in.
4 in.

_____

2.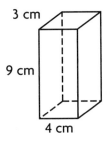
3 cm
9 cm
4 cm

_____

3.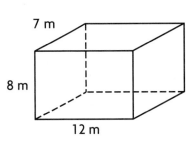
7 m
8 m
12 m

_____

Algebra Find the unknown dimension.

4. length = 11 yd

  width = 5 yd

  height = _____

  Volume = 165 yd^3

5. length = 14 ft

  width = 9 ft

  height = 4 ft

  Volume = _____

6. length = 8 in.

  width = _____

  height = 9 in.

  Volume = 288 in.^{3}

7. length = 5 cm

  width = 3 cm

  height = 15 cm

  Volume = _____

8. length = 6 yd

  width = 8 yd

  height = _____

  Volume = 288 yd^3

9. length = _____

  width = 11 in.

  height = 5 in.

  Volume = 385 in.^{3}

10. length = 15 in.

  width = 8 in.

  height = 2 in.

  Volume = _____

11. length = 6.5 m

  width = _____

  height = 2.5 m

  Volume = 65 yd^3

12. length = _____

  width = $5\frac{1}{2}$ ft

  height = $3\frac{1}{4}$ ft

  Volume = 143 ft^3

Mixed Review

13. Margie bought 8 cans of tomato soup and 4 cans of mushroom soup. She spent nine dollars and eighty-eight cents. The tomato soup cost $0.79 per can. What did the mushroom soup cost per can?

_____

14. Tom wants to buy a stereo that costs $540.00. He has saved $\frac{1}{3}$ of the cost. How much has Tom saved?

_____

Measure Perimeter, Area, and Volume

Tell the appropriate units to measure each. Write *units, square units,* or *cubic units.*

1. space in a cabinet

2. space in an oven

3. tile for a floor

_____   _____   _____

4. a wallpaper border

5. paper to cover a box

6. fence for a garden

_____   _____   _____

Write the units you would use to measure each.

7.
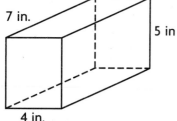
7 in.
5 in
4 in.

volume of this prism

_____

8.
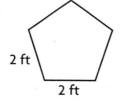
2 ft
2 ft

perimeter of this figure

_____

9.
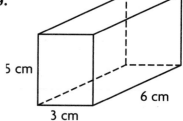
5 cm
6 cm
3 cm

surface area of this prism

_____

10.
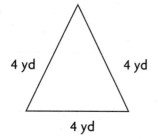
4 yd   4 yd
4 yd

area of this figure

_____

11.
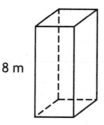
8 m

volume of this prism

_____

12.
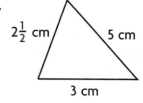
$2\frac{1}{2}$ cm   5 cm
3 cm

area of this figure

_____

Mixed Review

Evaluate.

13. $(27 - n) + 9$ if $n = 19$

14. $(n \times 5) - 6$ if $n = 7$

_____   _____

Problem Solving Skill: Use a Formula

Use a formula and solve.

1. A garden that is 18 feet wide and 22 feet long needs to be fenced. Will 25 yards of fencing be enough? Explain.

   _____

   _____

2. The trailer of a lumber truck is 15 feet wide, 18 feet long, and 10 feet high. Is the truck large enough to carry 2,500 cubic feet of lumber?

   _____

   _____

3. Tim has a box that is 18 inches long and 12 inches wide and has a volume of 3,240 cubic inches. He wants to pack an object that is 9 inches long, 6 inches wide, and 16 inches high. Will the object fit in the box? Explain.

   _____

   _____

   _____

   _____

4. New flooring is being installed in the school foyer. The area is 15 feet wide and 33 feet long. How many square yards of flooring are needed? What is the perimeter of the foyer, measured in feet? Explain how you found your answers.

   _____

   _____

   _____

   _____

Mixed Review

Solve.

5. Classes at the high school begin at 7:45 A.M. Each class is 50 minutes long, and there is a 7-minute break after each class. At what time does the second class of the day end?

   _____

6. A swimming pool is 60 feet long and 30 feet wide. How many cubic feet of water will be needed to fill the pool to a depth of 8 feet?

   _____

Understand Ratios

Vocabulary

Fill in the blank.

1. A _____ is a comparison of two quantities.

Write each ratio and name the type of ratio.

2. There were 4 baseballs and 6 basketballs.

    _____

3. Margo had 3 quarters and 2 pennies.

    _____

4. Math is preferred to science by 19 of 20 students.

    _____

5. Of 20 students, 11 are boys.

    _____

Write each ratio.

6. wings to planes

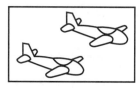 _____

7. flowers to stem

 _____

8. legs to spiders

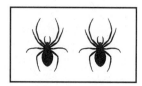 _____

9. fingers to hands

 _____

Mixed Review

Write each fraction in simplest form.

10. $\frac{12}{24}$

11. $\frac{6}{9}$

12. $\frac{28}{49}$

13. $\frac{96}{144}$

14. $\frac{40}{45}$

_____   _____   _____   _____   _____

Express Ratios

Write each ratio in three ways. Then name the type of ratio. Use the table below.

1. race games to sports games

_____

2. all games to arcade games

_____

3. sports games to all games

_____

Ben's Video Game Collection	
Type of Game	Number of Games
Race	5
Arcade	3
Sports	2

Circle *a* or *b* to show which fraction represents each ratio.

4. 7 to 9

   a. $\frac{9}{7}$ **b.** $\frac{7}{9}$

5. 6:2

   a. $\frac{6}{2}$ **b.** $\frac{2}{6}$

6. 9:3

   a. $\frac{9}{3}$ **b.** $\frac{3}{9}$

7. 11 to 16

   a. $\frac{16}{11}$ **b.** $\frac{11}{16}$

For 8–10, use the circle graph. Write each ratio in three ways.

8. What is the ratio of pictures to records?

_____

9. What is the ratio of pictures to all collectibles?

_____

10. What is the ratio of figurines to all collectibles?

_____

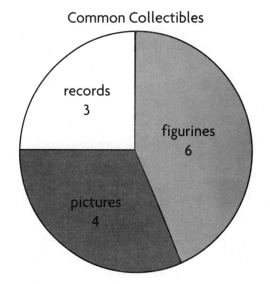

Common Collectibles

records 3

figurines 6

pictures 4

Mixed Review

11. What is the value of 3^4 ?

_____

12. Erik discovered he was $\frac{3}{4}$ as tall as Wilt Chamberlain, the basketball player. Chamberlain is 86 inches tall. How tall is Erik?

_____

Name _____

Ratios and Proportions

Vocabulary

Fill in the blank.

1. _____ are ratios that name the same amount.

2. A _____ is an equation that shows two equivalent ratios.

Tell whether the following ratios are equivalent. Write *yes* or *no*.

3. $\frac{3}{8}$ and $\frac{9}{24}$ 4. 4:5 and 5:4   5. 7 to 4 and 28 to 16

_____   _____   _____

6. $\frac{8}{4}$ and $\frac{2}{1}$ 7. 6:8 and 2:4   8. 3 to 15 and 4 to 20

_____   _____   _____

Write three ratios that are equivalent to the given ratio.

9. 7:1   10. 6:3

_____   _____

11. 3 to 2   12. $\frac{13}{15}$

_____   _____

Complete the ratio table.

13.

Number of oranges to make orange juice	5	___	___	___
Pints of orange juice	1	2	3	4

Tell whether the ratios form a proportion. Write *yes* or *no*.

14. $\frac{3}{4} = \frac{6}{12}$ _____   15. $\frac{8}{3} = \frac{24}{9}$ _____   16. $\frac{3}{6} = \frac{15}{30}$ _____

Mixed Review

17. $9\overline{)36.36}$ 18. $3\overline{)158.67}$ 19. $7\overline{)588.42}$ 20. $5\overline{)0.180}$ 21. $6\overline{)53.652}$

PW156   Practice

Scale Drawings

Vocabulary

Fill in the blank.

1. A ratio that compares the distance on a map to the

   actual distance is a _____.

Complete the ratio table.

2. Scale Distance (in.)	1	2	_____	7	_____
3. Actual Length (ft)	18	36	90	_____	198

4. Scale Distance (cm)	1	4	7	_____	15
5. Actual Length (m)	7	28	_____	84	_____

For 6–9, use the drawing of the patio and the scale.

6. What is the width of the pool in units?

   _____

7. What is the actual width of the pool?

   _____

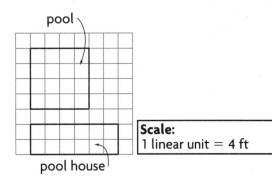

pool

pool house

Scale:
1 linear unit = 4 ft

8. What is the perimeter of the pool house in units? in feet?

   _____

9. What is the ratio of linear units to feet?

   _____

Mixed Review

10. How much fabric will Fran have left from a 20-yd bolt after cutting off $5\frac{1}{2}$ yd?

    _____

11. Miguel's yard is 28 ft long and 36 ft wide. It costs $0.50 per square foot to have grass planted. What is the total cost?

    _____

Problem Solving Skill

Too Much/Too Little Information

For 1–4, use this table. Write whether each problem has *too much* or *too little* information. Then solve if possible, or describe the additional information needed.

1. How many students are there in the fourth grade for every lunch buyer?

   _____

2. How many adult buyers are there for every buyer in fifth grade?

   _____

Who Buys Lunch?	
Grade	**Whole Class:Buyers**
3	110:55
4	96:32
5	116:80
6	108:84

3. What is the ratio of school population to lunch buyers?

   _____

4. What is the ratio of lunch buyers in grades 3 through 5 to all students in those grades?

   _____

Charneta loves a puppy at the pet store. His name is Beau, and he's a German shepherd. Beau costs $175.00. Charneta will work at Mr. Taylor's store for $6.00 an hour, sweeping floors and stocking shelves. How many hours will Charneta have to work to buy the dog?

5. What information is necessary to solve the problem?

   A the name of the dog

   B what kind of work Charneta will do

   C how much she will earn an hour

   D the store owner's age

6. What is the least number of hours Charneta can work in order to buy the dog?

   F 30 hours

   G 39 hours

   H 40 hours

   J 41 hours

Mixed Review

7. $22.21
   + 78.99

8. $47.50
   × 1.50

9. 32.498
   − 17.020

10. 156.52
    + 819.75

Understand Percent

Model each ratio. Then write the percent.

1. 67 cents out of 1 dollar

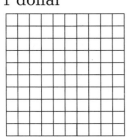

_____

2. 16 sheep out of 100 animals

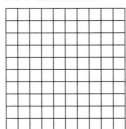

_____

3. 58 girls out of 100 children

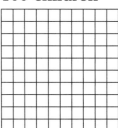

_____

Write a percent to describe the shaded part.

4.

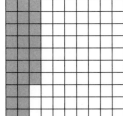

Percent _____

5.

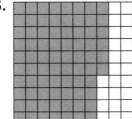

Percent _____

6.

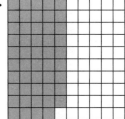

Percent _____

Choose the more reasonable percent. Circle *a* or *b*.

7. "*About half* the students bring their own lunches to school," said the cafeteria worker.

   a. 48 percent

   b. 85 percent

8. "*Very few* children are sent to the principal's office," said the teacher.

   a. 98 percent

   b. 2 percent

Mixed Review

Write as a decimal and a fraction.

9. thirty-nine hundredths

10. forty-four hundredths

_____

_____

Relate Decimals and Percents

Newly Acquired Library Books

For 1–4, use the circle graph. Write a decimal and a percent to describe each.

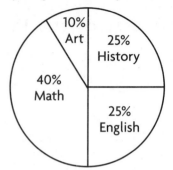

1. What part of the library books are art books?

_____

2. What part of the library books are English books?

_____

3. What part of the library books are not history books?

_____

4. What part of the library books are not math books?

_____

Write the number as a decimal and a percent.

5. sixty–four hundredths

_____

6. ninety–three hundredths

_____

7. fifteen hundredths

_____

8. thirty hundredths

_____

Write each decimal as a percent.

9. 0.46 _____

10. 0.79 _____

11. 0.20 _____

12. 0.03 _____

13. 0.18 _____

14. 0.86 _____

Write each percent as a decimal.

15. 38% _____

16. 74% _____

17. 2% _____

18. 16% _____

19. 22% _____

20. 91% _____

Mixed Review

21. $\begin{array}{r} 12 \\ \times\ 8 \\ \hline \end{array}$

22. $\begin{array}{r} 16 \\ \times\ 37 \\ \hline \end{array}$

23. $\begin{array}{r} 90 \\ \times\ 80 \\ \hline \end{array}$

24. $\begin{array}{r} 14 \\ \times\ 14 \\ \hline \end{array}$

25. $\begin{array}{r} 34 \\ \times\ 26 \\ \hline \end{array}$

Relate Fractions, Decimals, and Percents

Complete the tables. Write each fraction in simplest form.

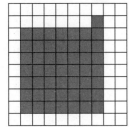

	Fraction	Decimal	Percent
1.			12%
3.	$\frac{3}{4}$		

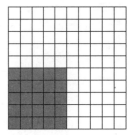

	Fraction	Decimal	Percent
2.	$\frac{17}{20}$		
4.			24%

Express the shaded part of each model as a decimal, a percent, and a fraction in simplest form.

5.

6.

7.

_____   _____   _____

Compare. Write $<$, $>$, or $=$ in each $\bigcirc$.

8. 11% $\bigcirc$ 0.11 9. 75% $\bigcirc$ $\frac{1}{3}$ 10. 15% $\bigcirc$ 1.5 11. 50% $\bigcirc$ 0.25

Tell whether each fraction or decimal is greater than 100% or between 1% and 100%. Write *greater* or *between*.

12. $\frac{600}{100}$ 13. $\frac{1}{2}$ 14. 6.9 15. $\frac{1}{8}$

_____   _____   _____   _____

Mixed Review

Find the sum, product, or difference.

16. $294,432$
    $+126,008$

17. $9,009$
    $\times\ 621$

18. $237,432$
    $-\ 49,163$

19. $241,430$
    $+798,790$

20. $6,855$
    $\times\ 530$

21. $257,743$
    $-\ 68,889$

Find a Percent of a Number

Find the percent of the number.

1. 5% of 50 _____   2. 15% of 45 _____   3. 35% of 42 _____

4. 200% of 80 _____   5. 150% of 20 _____   6. 65% of 150 _____

7. 60% of 93 _____   8. 60% of 60 _____   9. 150% of 75 _____

10. 25% of 200 _____   11. 2% of 48 _____   12. 40% of 150 _____

You can find the sales tax for any item you buy by finding a percent
of the price. Find the sales tax for each price to the nearest cent.

13. price: $9.75   14. price: $101.40   15. price: $172.00   16. price: $63.99
    tax rate: 3%   tax rate: 6.5%   tax rate: 11%   tax rate: 8%

_____   _____   _____   _____

Mixed Review

17. How many dimes are in $28.00?

18. Is 1.314 greater than or less than 1.341?

_____   _____

19. At $0.45 per dozen, how many dozens of oranges can you buy for $1.35?

20. A poultry farmer bought 2,000 chicks at $0.45 each. What did he pay for the chicks?

_____   _____

21. A butcher charged $7.44 for a certain cut of meat at $0.96 per pound. What was the weight of the meat?

22. The local baseball team bought 10 bats at $18.00 each and 7 balls at $1.98 each. If the 9 players shared the costs equally, how much was each player's share?

_____   _____

23.   17   24. 42.5   25.   3.55   26.   170   27.   4,615
     × 0.8   × 1.6   × 20   × 2.9   × 0.88

Name _____

Mental Math: Percent of a Number

Use mental math to find the percent of each number.

1. 150% of 500

2. 60% of 100

3. 40% of 25

4. 30% of 280

_____ _____ _____ _____

5. 16% of 200

6. 150% of 300

7. 200% of 60

8. 95% of 300

_____ _____ _____ _____

9. 85% of 200

10. 10% of 50

11. 80% of 225

12. 55% of 200

_____ _____ _____ _____

13. 60% of 300

14. 70% of 400

15. 20% of 20

16. 70% of 300

_____ _____ _____ _____

17. 10% of 120

18. 30% of 180

19. 50% of 96

20. 100% of 300

_____ _____ _____ _____

Mixed Review

For 21–24, write each in two other forms.

21. one and four hundredths

22. three and six tenths

_____ _____

23. 101.79

24. 2.875

_____ _____

_____ _____

25. James earns $72.00 for 6 hours of work. If he earns the same amount each hour, how much does he earn for 4 hours of work? For 1 hour?

26. The GCF of 9 and another number is 3. The LCM is 36. What is the number?

_____ _____

27. $2.50 × 7 = _____

28. $39.90 × 2 = _____

Problem Solving Strategy

Make a Graph

Make a graph and solve.

1. Abigail surveyed the fifth-grade students to find out their favorite TV shows. She organized the data in the table below. What is the best way for her to display the data? Which TV show is most popular?

_____

FAVORITE TV SHOWS	
Show	Percent of Votes
Plimpton	20%
Queen of the Hill	40%
Atlas	10%
Harborwatch	10%
The Butler	20%

Mixed Review

Solve.

2. Tamala recorded the average temperature for 6 months. She recorded 48° in April, 59° in May, 69° in June, 76° in July, 74° in August, and 64° in September. How can she best show this data?

3. Mylan spent $3 on a magazine. He spent half of his remaining money on a video game. He then spent half of his remaining money on a book. He had $12 left. How much money did Mylan begin with?

4. A dog pen will be 18 feet long and 12 feet wide. One length will be formed by the side of a garage. How much fencing is needed for the other 3 sides?

5. There were 63 people in a hotel. Then 7 checked out, and 3 times that number checked in. How many people are in the hotel now?

Compare Data Sets

For 1–8, use the two circle graphs. Both families planned
a monthly budget for all their expenses.

PETERSON FAMILY BUDGET
($850 per month)

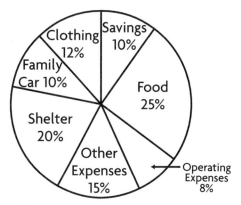

ASHLAND FAMILY BUDGET
($1,000 per month)

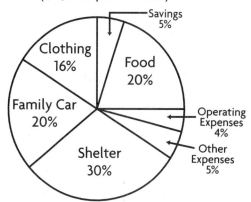

1. How much money did the
Peterson family spend on food on
a monthly basis?

_____

2. How much money did the
Ashland family spend on food
on a monthly basis?

_____

3. Which family put more money
into savings each month? how
much more?

_____

4. Which family paid more money
for shelter each month? how
much more?

_____

5. If the Peterson family income
increased by $50.00 per month
and the family kept the same
percents, how much would they
spend on clothing?

_____

6. If the Ashland family income
increased by $100 per month and
kept the same percents, how
much would they spend on other
expenses?

_____

7. What is the total budget of the
Peterson family for one year?

_____

8. What is the yearly budget for the
family car for the Ashland family?

_____

Mixed Review

9.   6.34
  − 5.13

10. $0.02 \overline{)12.8}$

11.   47.74
  − 33.83

12.   28.61
  + 95.75

Probability Experiments

Vocabulary

Fill in the blank.

1. A table of _____ shows
results that could occur.

Write the possible events.

2. rolling a cube labeled 12, 14, 16, 18, 20, 22

_____

3. spinning the pointer on a spinner with sections of red, blue, and yellow

_____

4. pulling a can from a grocery bag with 1 can of corn, 2 cans of beans, and 1 can of peas

_____

5. pulling a shape out of a bag that has 3 red squares, 2 blue squares, and 0 yellow squares

_____

6. tossing a coin with heads on one side and tails on the other

_____

7. pulling a marble from a bag that has 1 red, 2 green, and 1 yellow marble

_____

Mixed Review

Find the value of n.

8. $12 + 5 = n$ _____

9. $20 - n = 5$ _____

10. $n - 8 = 15$ _____

11. $6 + n = 11$ _____

12. $n + 14 = 28$ _____

13. $40 - n = 5$ _____

14. $10 \times n = 100$ _____

15. $n \times 7 = 28$ _____

16. $81 \div n = 9$ _____

17. $8 \times 2 = n$ _____

18. $45 \div n = 5$ _____

19. $n \times 9 = 27$ _____

Divide.

20. $14\overline{)126}$

21. $6\overline{)0.036}$

22. $17\overline{)289}$

23. $23\overline{)1{,}035}$

Outcomes

Vocabulary

Fill in the blank.

1. A _____ shows all the possible outcomes of an event.

Make a tree diagram to show the possible choices. Solve.

2. For a snack, Sue can have either an apple or a cheese slice. She can have either a glass of milk or a glass of grape juice. How many different snack choices does Sue have?

3. For breakfast, Jill can have either oat or wheat cereal. She can top the cereal with either raisins, bananas, strawberries, or blueberries. How many breakfast choices does Jill have?

4. Bill can make a picture with either paints or markers or both. He can use either construction paper or poster paper. How many different ways can Bill make a picture?

5. For gift wrapping, Elsa has a choice of either red, blue, pink, or orange paper. She has a choice of either red, blue, pink, or orange ribbon. How many different ways can Elsa wrap a gift?

Mixed Review

6. 4.01
  + 3.69

7. 6.905
  + 4.98

8. 9.463
  − 1.02

9. 16.5
  − 9.6

10. 28.06
  + 5.09

11. 7.35
  − 0.98

12. 7.150
  + 5.051

13. 0.108
  + 7.962

14. 0.54
  − 0.37

15. 5.982
  + 0.153

16. 19.71
  − 15.09

17. 6.118
  + 4.212

18. 31.407
  + 50.527

19. 18.3
  + 28.8

20. 6.3172
  − 1.0984

Probability Expressed as a Fraction

Vocabulary

Fill in the blanks.

1. _____ is the chance that an event will happen.

2. Each event is _____, or has the same chance of happening.

Write a fraction for the probability of pulling each color marble from a bag of 4 red, 1 green, 2 blue, and 3 yellow marbles.

3. green

4. red

5. orange

6. blue

_____   _____   _____   _____

Write a fraction for the probability of spinning each color on a spinner with 2 red, 3 yellow, 2 green, and 1 blue sections.

7. yellow

8. red

9. yellow or blue

10. blue

_____   _____   _____   _____

11. Angie is one of 30 girls trying out for the 12 positions on the basketball team. What is the probability that Angie will make the team?

12. Of 100 tickets available for the school raffle, Tom bought 3, Jack bought 5, and Mark bought 2. What is the probability of each boy winning?

_____

_____

_____

_____

Mixed Review

13. $3.2\overline{)653}$

14. $(7 \times 6) + (3 \times \frac{1}{2}) = n$

15. $\frac{1}{6} \div \frac{1}{2}$

_____   _____   _____

16. $(7 \times 4) - (2.5 \times 2) = n$

17. $\frac{2}{5} \times \frac{4}{3}$

18. $329 - (12 \times 11) = n$

_____   _____   _____

Name _____

Compare Probabilities

For 1–6, use a bag of 3 red, 5 blue, 4 yellow, and 3 green buttons. Write each probability as a fraction. Tell which event is more likely.

1. You pull a yellow button. _____

You pull a red button. _____

More likely _____

2. You pull a blue button. _____

You pull a green button. _____

More likely _____

3. You pull a red or yellow button.

_____

You pull a green or blue button.

_____

More likely _____

4. You pull a blue button.

_____

You pull a black button.

_____

More likely _____

5. You pull a button that isn't

green. _____

You pull a button that isn't

yellow. _____

More likely _____

6. You pull a button that isn't red.

_____

You pull a button that isn't blue.

_____

More likely _____

7. Joey had 2 pairs of red socks, 4 pairs of black socks, and 12 pairs of white socks. What is the probability that he will pull a pair of black socks from his drawer?

_____

8. Raimondo has pizza once a week for dinner. What is the probability that he will have pizza for dinner tonight?

_____

Mixed Review

9. $35.6\overline{)2{,}071.92}$

10. $\frac{1}{2} \times \frac{5}{6} =$

11. $3\frac{1}{3} \div \frac{1}{6} =$

Problem Solving Strategy

Make an Organized List

Make an organized list to solve.

1. Aber is conducting a probability experiment with a number cube and two marbles. The cube is numbered 1–6. One marble is red, the other blue. How many possible outcomes are there for this experiment? What is the probability for getting 1 and blue?

2. Mark feeds his cat a cup of dry food and a can of wet food every day. The dry food is either chicken or fish flavored. The wet food is either tuna, salmon, or beef. List all the possible combinations of wet and dry cat food. What is the probability of picking chicken?

Mixed Strategy Practice

Solve.

3. In the school election, Dave received 38 percent of the vote, Marcia received 41 percent, and Claudia received 21 percent. What type of graph would Dave use to display the data?

4. Estelle uses the numbers 3, 5, and 7 to write two-digit numbers without repeating any digits in the same number. List her numbers.

5. Martha has 6 coins that are quarters, dimes, and nickels. She has a total of $0.80. What combination of coins does she have?

6. At the movies, Jorge spent $0.95 on soda and $2.25 on popcorn. The ticket cost $4.50. If he has $2.30 left, how much money did Jorge have to begin with?